THE BRITISH COMMUNIST PARTY

THE BRITISH COMMUNIST PARTY

A HISTORICAL PROFILE

BY

HENRY PELLING

FELLOW OF THE QUEEN'S COLLEGE, OXFORD

ADAM AND CHARLES BLACK

LONDON

FIRST PUBLISHED 1958

A. AND C. BLACK LTD
4, 5 AND 6 SOHO SQUARE, LONDON W.1

© HENRY PELLING 1958

PRINTED IN GREAT BRITAIN
BY ROBERT CUNNINGHAM AND SONS LTD, ALVA

ONULP

PREFACE

THE British Communist Party, a section of the Communist International from 1920 until the dissolution of the International in 1943, was known in that period as the Communist Party of Great Britain (C.P.G.B.); and as such, apart from various commitments in supporting parties abroad and in encouraging the development of those 'within the sphere of British imperialism', its direct activity has normally been confined to Great Britain and does not include any part of Ireland.

In preparing the present work I must acknowledge the assistance of some present and many former members of the party, and also of former members of foreign Communist parties. A few of them would perhaps be embarrassed if I mentioned their names here; and for that reason I do not do so, though none the less grateful for their help.

I have also received valuable advice from various academic colleagues. I must in particular name Mr Theodore Draper, Dr Mark Abrams, Mrs Jane Degras, Mr R. N. Carew Hunt, and Dr Ivan Avakumovic. Dr Avakumovic and Mr R. A. C. Parker did me the kindness of reading the typescript and making a number of useful suggestions for its improvement. None of these colleagues is in any way responsible for the interpretation of Communist history which I have adopted, or for the errors of fact which may remain.

Contemporary studies have special problems, but also special opportunities. I should much welcome hearing from any readers who are in a position to throw fresh light on the events herein recorded, either by the loan of documents or by personal reminiscence. I should then be able to correct and supplement this analysis of what has previously been a very obscure aspect of recent history.

H. M. P.

Oxford, June 1958

NOTE ON SPECIAL ABBREVIATIONS

The following special abbreviations have been used in the footnotes and in Appendix A:

CI	Communist International
CP	Communist Party of Great Britain
DW	*Daily Worker*
ECCI	Executive Committee, Communist International
Inprecorr	*International Press Correspondence*
RILU	Red International of Labour Unions
WN	*World News*
WNV	*World News and Views*

CONTENTS

ILLUSTRATIONS

CHAPTER I

ORIGINS AND FOUNDATION

THE members of the British Communist Party have often claimed – at some times more vehemently than at others – that they represent the culmination of a long radical tradition, running from the Levellers, through men like Cartwright and Tom Paine and the Chartists, to Socialists of the late nineteenth century such as William Morris. It is true enough that there has been a long tradition of radicalism in Britain, and, for well over a century, something of a Socialist tradition as well: and the Communist Party can fairly make a claim to a share – though certainly not a monopoly – of these in the present. But the Communists are in many ways set apart from all British antecedents by their most distinctive feature – their disciplined adherence to Marxist-Leninist theory. For Lenin spent only a short time in England, and Marx, in spite of many years of residence, made no attempt to assimilate himself to British ways, and preferred to think and write in German.

To begin with Marx. Both he and his collaborator Engels wrote their works of political and economic analysis in German, and Marx's most important work, the first volume of *Capital*, though published in German in 1857, was not translated into English until 1886. Even Engels's *Condition of the Working Class in England in 1844*, published in Leipzig in 1845, did not appear in English until 1887, and then under the imprint of an American house. The founders of the first British Marxist organisation at the beginning of the eighteen-eighties, the Social-Democratic Federation (S.D.F.), had read *Capital* in French: but according to Marx and Engels themselves, they did not really understand the new doctrine that they had adopted. They made a shibboleth of the Marxian Theory of Value, which figures prominently in the first volume of *Capital*, but paid little attention to many of Marx's other ideas. Engels described H. M. Hyndman, who was for many years the principal leader of the S.D.F., as 'an arch-Conservative', and 'extremely chauvinistic'[1]; and he spoke of William Morris patronisingly as 'all very well as far as he goes, but it is not far', and 'a settled sentimental Socialist'.[2] If this was the impression made upon him by the leading British Marxists, what could he hope for from the men who were to dominate British labour politics in the following generation – men like Keir Hardie, Ramsay MacDonald, Philip Snowden and Arthur Henderson? The British political climate was indeed profoundly uncongenial both to Marx and Engels; and when Engels died in 1895, having outlived his old friend and colleague by a dozen years, the S.D.F., tiny as it was by comparison with continental Socialist parties, seemed to have been left high and dry out of the main stream of British labour politics.

Yet the Marxist influence did not die out in Britain, although it constantly needed fresh transfusions of strength from abroad. It seems ironical today to reflect that the major influence in reviving British Marxism at the turn of the century came from America. Just over fifty years ago Marxian Socialism began to develop rapidly in the United States, where industry was mushrooming into enormous trusts and corporations which seemed to foreshadow the 'expropriation of the expropriators' of which Marx had spoken, and where great hosts of immigrants from Central and Eastern Europe remained as yet unassimilated and on the verge of destitution. Daniel De Leon, according to Lenin the only American to make an original contribution to Marxist theory,[3] took the lead of a 'Socialist Labor Party' which sponsored a flow of translations of Marxist classics and evolved a theory of revolution by industrial action – not so much by using the existing trade unions, which in America were small, conservative craft societies, but by starting afresh with One Big Union to embrace all workers and to be called the Industrial Workers of the World. De Leon's ideas provoked a response in Britain among a genera-

[1] To Bebel, 30 Aug. 1883, *Selected Correspondence of Marx and Engels* (1936), p. 419.
[2] *Correspondance Engels-Lafargue* (Paris, 1956), i, 174 and 379.
[3] See the evidence quoted by Henry Kuhn in the symposium, *Daniel De Leon* (New York, 1920), i, 79 and 81.

tion which was too young to have been influenced by the first wave of Marxism in the eighteen-eighties; and especially among those who were distrustful of attempts to use Parliament as a means to reform. This attitude was most noticeable in the industrial areas of Scotland and Wales, where there was a traditional suspicion of English political institutions. It was not accidental, therefore, that a 'Socialist Labour Party' (S.L.P.) appeared on Clydeside as a secession from the S.D.F., and that the Plebs League and the Labour College movement, which were also expressions of the same De Leonite influence, struck their deepest roots among the South Wales miners.[1] Against the background of British society as a whole, this second wave of Marxism had only a minute effect; but in particular areas it produced a nucleus of working-class Marxists who, in periods of widespread discontent, could provide a significant political leadership.

It was the First World War which occasioned such a period of discontent and, largely as a result of the Russian Revolution, set in motion a third wave of Marxist influence in Britain. It was to be expected that industrial Scotland and Wales, where sectional factors were strongest, should again be the areas most affected. Consequently, the members of the S.L.P. were naturally in the lead. But the membership of the old S.D.F., now somewhat expanded under the new name of British Socialist Party (B.S.P.), also had its part to play. The first two years of the war saw a bitter conflict inside the B.S.P. between the supporters and opponents of the war – the former, though less numerous, being for the most part the more senior members of the party, led by H. M. Hyndman himself. The climax of the struggle came at the annual conference in 1916, when Hyndman and his supporters were defeated and retired from the organisation, leaving it free to take a firm line of opposition to the war.[2]

To assist the war effort, the Labour Party had agreed to an election truce, and the trade-union leaders had promised to accept many restrictions of normal union practice. This was the oppor-

---

[1] For De Leonite influence in Britain, see C. Tsuzuki, 'The Impossibilist Revolt in Britain', *International Review of Social History*, i (1956), 377-97.

[2] H. W. Lee and E. Archbold, *Social-Democracy in Britain* (1935), pp. 236-9.

tunity for the Marxist opposition to make itself felt in the industrial sphere. On Clydeside, a Workers' Committee was formed in 1915, led by such men as Arthur MacManus and Tom Bell of the S.L.P. and John Maclean and Willie Gallacher of the B.S.P. With the exception of Maclean who was a school-teacher (and, incidentally, one of the best-known Marxist propagandists of the time), these men were all employed in industry.[1] Strikes and rioting on the Clyde soon demonstrated their success; and in 1917 the government endeavoured to break the Committee's power by exiling its leaders to other parts of Britain. The result was the reverse of what was intended: the movement began to assume a nation-wide character, and in August 1917 a National Committee of Shop Stewards was set up.[2] Meanwhile a more or less independent struggle was being waged in South Wales by the militant 'Unofficial Reform Committee', which continued to grow in strength at the expense of the old leaders.[3] Thus on the eve of the Bolshevik Revolution in Russia, Marxist revolutionaries in Britain were increasingly successful in focussing the industrial discontents of wartime.

The first Russian Revolution, in March 1917, was the Liberal revolution that put Kerensky in power; and it was not merely the Marxists in Britain who hailed its accomplishment. Socialists and Liberals of all complexions greeted the overthrow of Czarism as a good augury for the future, and hoped that it was the first step on the way to a peace on democratic principles. In the first flush of enthusiasm even Ramsay MacDonald and Philip Snowden were to be heard uttering revolutionary phrases in sympathy with the Russians.[4] But in November Kerensky's régime was overthrown by Lenin and the Bolsheviks, and the general approval of the Russian Revolution on the British Left began to dwindle. Lenin, who was the theoretician as well as the practical leader of his

[1] See W. Gallacher, *Revolt on the Clyde* (1936); Tom Bell, *Pioneering Days* (1941) and *John Maclean* (Glasgow, 1944).

[2] For an early account of the movement, see J. T. Murphy in Arthur Gleason's *What the Workers Want* (New York, 1920), pp. 184ff.

[3] 'Commission of Enquiry into Industrial Unrest in Wales', *Parliamentary Papers* 1917-18, xv, 105.

[4] See Leeds convention report, *Labour Leader*, 7 June 1917.

party, had developed the Marxian idea of the dictatorship of the proletariat to mean – for a time at least – the dictatorship of a minority party of disciplined revolutionaries. Such a course of action was alien to the thinking of the Labour Party leaders in Britain, and they showed their feelings at once by allowing the exiled Kerensky to address their annual conference in June 1918.[1] It is true that the British Government's attempts to intervene in Russia were opposed by the great bulk of the Labour Party, and that the 'Hands off Russia' Campaign owed its success in halting British intervention to the threat of direct action by the unions, under such leaders as Ernest Bevin. But those who were prepared to accept the new Marxist-Leninist type of revolutionary theory as suitable for British conditions turned out to be few more than the S.L.P. and B.S.P. Marxists, who had long been fighting against the big battalions of the Labour Party and the trade unions.

*   *   *

In January 1919 the Russian Bolsheviks announced the formation of a Communist International (Comintern), and invited sympathetic organisations throughout the world to send delegates to a conference in Russia in March.[2] At this time the revolution was still very much on the defensive, being blockaded and attacked on all sides by White Russian and Allied forces. Hardly any parties or groups in countries not already inside the Soviet sphere could send delegates, and no specially-appointed representatives from Britain could attend.[3] But the British left-wing groups realised the significance of the occasion, and began to consider how they could consolidate themselves into a Communist Party, so as to become a component of the new International. Serious differences existed among them, chiefly on the question of the importance to be attached to parliamentary action as a means of reform. The B.S.P. attached so much importance to this that it had re-affiliated to the Labour Party in 1916. The S.L.P.

[1] Labour Party *Eighteenth Annual Report* 1918, pp. 35, 60f.

[2] J. Degras (ed.), *Communist International 1919-43, Documents*, i (1956), pp. 1-5.

[3] One J. Fineberg, a member of the B.S.P. who moved to Russia in 1918, was regarded as the spokesman for Britain. See *Der I. Kongress der Kommunistischen Internationale: Protokoll der Verhandlungen* (Hamburg, 1921), p. 5.

was somewhat divided: although some of its prominent members had stood as candidates in the 1918 General Election, the party tradition was largely one of industrial action to secure political ends. The opposition to parliamentary action in the S.L.P. ranks had its counterpart in the leadership of the Shop Stewards and Workers' Committee. Sylvia Pankhurst, of the famous suffragette family, who ran an independent body in East London called the Workers' Socialist Federation, was also to be reckoned among the British revolutionaries who abhorred the idea of parliamentary action.

It was Sylvia Pankhurst who took the initiative among the British sympathisers of Bolshevism, by getting in direct touch with Lenin. Immediately after the foundation of the new International she wrote to tell him of the existing divisions among the British Marxists, and to ask his opinion about the controversial question of parliamentary action.[1] Her letter was dated 16th July 1919 and it elicited a full and careful response dated 28th August. Lenin, the supreme opportunist, was in favour of the use of any and every method of attaining power, but he was not anxious to alienate any of the British Marxist groups. The key passage of his letter read:

> I am personally convinced that to renounce participation in the parliamentary elections is a mistake for the revolutionary workers of England, but better to make that mistake than to delay the formation of a big workers' Communist Party in England.[2]

In the then critical situation of the Bolshevik régime, it was evident that Lenin was anxious above all to see unity among the Bolshevik sympathisers inside Britain.

Meanwhile, the Communist International itself had issued an official summons to the British groups to drop their differences and form a united party.[3] From the outset, the formation of the British Communist organisation differed from that of the other major European countries, in that it was a question of assembling together a number of tiny left-wing groups, rather than of seeking to win the bulk or a large part of the main working-class move-

[1] Printed in *Communist International*, no. 5 (1919), pp. 5of.
[2] *Lenin on Britain* (1934), p. 244.   [3] B.S.P. *Conference Report*, 1920, p. 42.

ment. The Labour Party, dominated as it was by official trade unionism, could not conceivably be won over in the short run; even the Independent Labour Party, the major British Socialist group, which had a fine internationalist tradition, had been insufficiently influenced by Marxism to provide many recruits for Leninism. The largest prospective component of the new Communist organisation was the British Socialist Party, which had affiliated to the Labour Party on a supposed membership of 10,000, although in reality its paid-up membership was probably only about a quarter of this total.[1] All the other groups which could be expected to merge with the B.S.P. probably could not muster as many as this between them. However, as was often the case with Socialist organisations, their weakness seemed to increase the doctrinal intransigence of their leaders, rather than to reduce it.

The B.S.P., which as the largest of the groups concerned had least to lose by unity, summoned a series of meetings of representatives, which started in June 1919, and dragged on into the spring of the following year.[2] At first it seemed that a basis of unity had been found by leaving the question of Labour Party affiliation to be settled by referendum of the united membership after the formation of the new party. The S.L.P. delegates – Bell, MacManus, and J. T. Murphy, all of whom had been prominent in the wartime industrial struggles – agreed to these terms, but they were disavowed by their executive committee. This led to a split in the S.L.P. organisation: Bell, MacManus and Murphy decided to go on with the negotiations, although they now represented only a minority. But in the new situation Sylvia Pankhurst decided to withdraw, apparently to avoid being overwhelmed by the B.S.P. on the question of parliamentary action. She summoned a special conference of her own in June 1920 at which, with a few outside sympathisers, she changed the name of her Workers' Socialist Federation into 'Communist Party (British Section of the Third International)'.[3]

Sylvia Pankhurst's sudden adoption of the 'Communist' title

[1] Bell, *Pioneering Days*, pp. 194f.
[2] For an account of the negotiations see B.S.P. *Conference Report*, 1920, pp. 42-44.   [3] *Workers' Dreadnought*, 26 June 1920.

was clearly designed to queer the pitch for the advocates of parliamentary action. But the latter were not so easily defeated, numbering as they did not only the great bulk of the B.S.P. but also several prominent leaders from the S.L.P. They therefore formed a 'Unity Committee' with four representatives each of the B.S.P. and the S.L.P. group, and published a general invitation to a 'Unity Convention' to be held at the end of July. Delegates were to be admitted to the Convention only from organisations which accepted 'the fundamental basis of Communist Unity: (a) the Dictatorship of the Working Class; (b) the Soviet System; (c) the Third International'.[1] Nothing was said in the invitation about the controversial questions of parliamentary action and affiliation to the Labour Party.

The Unity Committee also decided to consult Lenin on the Pankhurst affair. Their letter, dated 20th June, received a reply in the following month, in which Lenin criticised Sylvia Pankhurst's policy as 'wrong' and repeated his own opinion: 'I personally am in favour of participation in Parliament and of adhesion to the Labour Party on condition of free and independent Communist activity.'[2] With this endorsement from the architect of the new Russia, the impending Unity Convention naturally assumed greater importance, although the executive of the S.L.P., as well as Sylvia Pankhurst and her associates, would have nothing to do with it.

Some one hundred and fifty delegates were in attendance when the Convention opened on 31st July at the Cannon Street Hotel – a railway hotel just east of St Paul's Cathedral, which had rooms available for stockholders' meetings and the like. These unfamiliar surroundings did not overawe the delegates, but at the end of the day the Convention had to be adjourned and was carried on for a further day in the doubtless more congenial atmosphere of the International Socialist Club in the East Road. The chairman was Arthur MacManus, formerly of the S.L.P.; but three-fifths of the delegates represented branches of the B.S.P., as against only one-sixth from S.L.P. branches. The remainder were accredited by

[1] *Communist Unity Convention Report*, 1920, p. 3.
[2] *Lenin on Britain*, p. 261.

local independent Socialist societies, Shop Stewards and Workers' committees, Guild Socialist groups, and so on.

MacManus, a diminutive but sharp-tongued Clydeside Irishman, the son of a Fenian, himself with a remarkable record of leadership in industrial unrest and resistance to the wartime government, was the right man to set the tone of the occasion. 'We believe', he said,

> that a social revolution is absolutely essential, and that it is our duty to get it however much we may be soiled in the process. Even if there arises a necessity for bloodshed, we can always remember that the lesson of history is that it is never the revolutionary who is responsible for the shedding of blood; it is invariably the counter-revolutionary.[1]

After these brave words, which undoubtedly expressed the general view of the delegates, the Convention got down to business. The first resolution was universally acceptable, repeating as it did one of the conditions of the delegates' admission, approval of the system of government by Soviets. A. A. Purcell, a member of the Parliamentary Committee of the T.U.C., and the most prominent trade unionist to belong to the B.S.P., moved to approve 'the Soviet or Workers' Council system as a system whereby the working class shall achieve power and take control of the forces of production'. This was carried unanimously.[2]

There followed a long debate on the subject of parliamentary action, which, in spite of the absence of the bulk of the S.L.P. and Sylvia Pankhurst's group, did not commend itself to all the delegates. In the end, however, it was approved by a majority of about ten to one.[3] The even thornier question of affiliation to the Labour Party, which was taken on the second day of the Convention, found a minority of the B.S.P. in alliance with nearly all the representatives of other bodies, and the resolution in favour of affiliation was carried by only a small majority – 100 to 85.[4] In reaching these decisions, Lenin's pamphlet *Left Wing Communism, an Infantile Disorder*, which had just been published, must have had its effect on the delegates: it was mentioned by the proposer of

---

[1] *Communist Unity Convention Report*, 1920, p. 5.
[2] *Ibid.*, pp. 6-9. [3] *Ibid.*, p. 21. [4] *Ibid.*, p. 57.

B

the affiliation resolution, J. F. Hodgson of the B.S.P., and although another speaker, William Paul of the S.L.P., protested that 'Lenin is no Pope or God', the Russian leader's words were bound to carry weight, especially as some passages dealt specifically with the problem of the British party under discussion. The passing of the affiliation resolution did not, of course, imply any sympathy for the existing leaders of the Labour Party: as Lenin put it, the Communists ought to support Henderson 'as a rope supports the hanged'[1]; and a B.S.P. delegate who spoke in favour of affiliation summed up the task of the British Communists as

> first of all to help the Labour Party get into office, and then, when they have got into office, our first act is to kick them out.[2]

Since full unity had not yet been achieved, the provisional committee of eight members (four B.S.P., four S.L.P.) was instructed to carry on, with the addition of six persons elected by the Convention. Four of those elected were in fact B.S.P. members, including Colonel L'Estrange Malone, an M.P. who had been returned to Parliament in 1918 as a Liberal on the Lloyd George ticket, but who had joined the B.S.P. after a visit to Russia just after the November revolution. The two new committee members not of the B.S.P. were William Mellor, a young Oxford graduate who was on the staff of George Lansbury's left-wing journal, the *Herald*; and Bob Stewart, of Dundee, who was the leader of the Socialist Prohibition Fellowship. The B.S.P. thus had a clear majority on the new executive, and although Mac-Manus was its chairman, its secretary was Albert Inkpin, the secretary of the B.S.P. This was to be expected, as it was obvious that the basis of the new organisation could only be that provided by the national headquarters and branches of the B.S.P. Defying the possibility of confusion with Sylvia Pankhurst's new organisation, the committee assumed the title of Communist Party of Great Britain, and under that name on 10th August applied for affiliation to the Labour Party.[3]

*   *   *

---

[1] *Lenin on Britain*, p. 257.   [2] *Communist Unity Convention Report*, 1920, p. 41.
[3] Labour Party *Report*, 1921, pp. 18ff.

Thus by the summer of 1920 there were two British Communist Parties in existence, that founded by Sylvia Pankhurst and that brought into existence by the B.S.P.-S.L.P. Unity Committee; and outside both were those who controlled the S.L.P. executive in Scotland, as well as the members of sundry political or industrial groups without national affiliation. Meanwhile in Moscow the Second Congress of the Communist International was holding its sessions, and Lenin and his colleagues were making it one of their major tasks to convert the whole of the rather heterogeneous British delegation to the need for working through the Labour Party. The delegates included two leaders who were not easily overborne by Lenin's arguments – Sylvia Pankhurst herself, and Willie Gallacher, who represented the Scottish Workers' Committee, which was the successor of the old Clyde Workers' Committee. Gradually Lenin won these two round to the view that they must make fresh attempts to secure unity among the British supporters of the Russian Revolution. Although Sylvia Pankhurst apparently did not abandon her rooted opposition to political action, Willie Gallacher succumbed to the arguments of Lenin, which were expressed both on paper in *Left Wing Communism* and also in long discussions in the course of the Congress.[1]

In this process of conversion the atmosphere of the capital city of a revolutionary country undoubtedly played its part. How could the British Marxists, who were so much on the fringe of British politics, fail to be impressed by the fact that they were negotiating with the rulers of a vast nation? Few of the British delegates returned in a critical frame of mind, but one who did could sense the way his colleagues were reacting:

> It is fairly evident that to many Communists Russia is not a country to learn from, but a sacrosanct Holy of Holies to grovel before as a pious Mohammedan faces the Mecca in his prayers.[2]

However, now that Sylvia Pankhurst had been won over to a further attempt at unity, the centre of resistance among the Marxists lay in Scotland, where the bulk of the S.L.P. still stood

[1] Gallacher, *Revolt on the Clyde*, pp. 250-3.
[2] *Worker* (Glasgow), 2 Oct. 1920.

out, and where John Maclean, who had been appointed Bolshevik consul in Glasgow by the Soviet Government, was agitating for a separate Scottish Communist Party. It was perhaps fortunate for Gallacher, who had promised Lenin to do his best to rally the waverers, that the Communist application to affiliate to the Labour Party had been abruptly turned down by the Labour Party National Executive, who had naturally taken into account the highly opportunist arguments in favour of affiliation used by the Communists among themselves.[1] In October Gallacher, attending a conference in Glasgow of the various remaining revolutionary elements, persuaded the majority of them to follow his lead in seeking unity with the C.P.G.B. Although Maclean with a few personal supporters, together with a remnant of the S.L.P., still stood out, a Glasgow committee was now elected to negotiate for a further Unity Convention.[2]

The final unity negotiations took place in Leeds early in January 1921. MacManus and Inkpin, for the C.P.G.B., met representatives both of the Glasgow negotiating committee and of Sylvia Pankhurst's Communist Party: and they arranged to hold a fresh convention in Leeds at the end of the month. It was agreed, however, that elections for the new committee of the united party should be partly on a geographical basis and partly on the basis of representation for the participating groups.[3] Unity was thus to be limited by a measure of federalism, which clearly reflected the sectionalism that, as we have seen, was all along an important feature of the Marxist support in Britain.

The Second Unity Convention of the C.P.G.B. met at the Victory Hotel in Leeds on 29th January 1921. The manager of the hotel was surprised to find that he was providing hospitality for Communists: a member of the unity committee had booked the rooms in the name of the National Fruiterers' Association, giving the address in Covent Garden (No. 16, King Street) which the C.P.G.B. had secured for its headquarters.[4] According to Jack Jones, a Welsh miner, the delegates, who numbered about as many as at the earlier convention, were a highly heterogeneous

---

[1] Labour Party *Report*, 1921, pp. 19-22.   [2] *Worker*, 16 Oct. 1920.
[3] *Ibid.*, 22 Jan. 1921.   [4] *Leeds Mercury*, 1 Feb. 1921.

collection, and some of the more proletarian of them were inclined to look askance at professional men like Walton Newbold,
the journalist, who had formerly been in the I.L.P., and William
Mellor, the chairman of the Standing Orders Committee of the
convention, who seemed 'offensively patrician'.[1] Another account
speaks of the 'only moment of enthusiasm' on the first day when
the resolution fusing the three main component organisations was
carried: the delegates 'rose to their feet and spontaneously broke
into the "Internationale"'.[2] MacManus, who stood for the chairmanship of the enlarged C.P.G.B., easily defeated Gallacher, his
only opponent, who was the candidate of the Scottish group now
joining the party.[3] Sylvia Pankhurst, who was in prison and so
could not attend, was apparently not a candidate for office; and
Gallacher having stood for the chairmanship could not also be
nominated for the committee. But since the arrangements for
group and area representation on the committee now came into
effect, it could not be said that the different elements went un-
represented. Still, as Sylvia Pankhurst was the editor of a journal
(the *Workers' Dreadnought*) it was obvious that her relationship to
the officers of the party would be a problem. The question of the
future status of her paper was referred to the committee, which
already had one journal in the weekly *Communist* (formerly the
B.S.P. *Call*). Further, the existence of a fraternal delegate from
the 'I.L.P. Left' – a group of sympathisers who still hoped to win
over the I.L.P. to the Communist International – indicated that
comprehension of Communist elements was not yet complete.

At any rate, after this Second Unity Convention most of the
elements that Lenin had particularly wanted to unite were now in
one organisation. As MacManus said, 'The Communist Parties
are dead: long live the Communist Party.'[4] The Russian leader
must have heard of the Convention with a certain satisfaction and
perhaps a little pride: for was he not personally the architect of
unity? And, if the party was as yet small, who could tell how
much it might grow? Of its complete identification with the

[1] J. Jones, *Unfinished Journey* (1938), p. 193.   [2] *Solidarity*, 4 Feb. 1921.
[3] Gallacher, *Revolt on the Clyde*, p. 255; *Communist*, 5 Feb. 1921.
[4] *Worker*, 5 Feb. 1921.

Russian Bolsheviks there was no doubt: an agent of the Executive of the Communist International was greeted with acclamation when he revealed his presence at the Leeds meeting, and the Bolshevik anthem was again sung; and William Paul the very man who had spoken against turning Lenin into 'a Pope or God', declared in the course of the proceedings that they were all animated by 'a breath of Moscow, a breath from the East, where there is wisdom'.[1]

But the 'wisdom of Moscow' was not yet widely appreciated in Britain. As the convention dispersed, a number of the delegates remained behind for discussion and conviviality. Some of them, flushed with a combination of alcohol and revolutionary enthusiasm, struck up the 'Red Flag' and the 'Internationale' in the hotel bar. Other guests of the hotel, mostly commercial travellers, retaliated with 'God Save the King' and cries of 'Clear out to Moscow'. The situation was threatening to turn into a riot, when a member of the executive – perhaps feeling guilty about the subterfuge adopted to book accommodation in the first place – went round the Communists urging them to return to their rooms or to hasten off home. They obeyed: it was their first act of discipline in an organisation where discipline was to count for almost everything.[2]

[1] *Worker*, 5 Feb. 1921.   [2] Jones, *op. cit.*, p. 196.

CHAPTER II

'BOLSHEVISATION', 1921-4

THE organisations that had now merged themselves in the nascent
C.P.G.B. were, as Lenin said, 'all very weak and some very, very
weak'.[1] At the Third Congress of the Comintern in 1921 a claim
of 10,000 members was made for the British Party – probably
based on the figure used by the B.S.P. for its affiliation to the
Labour Party.[2] In fact, however, it was an exaggeration, perhaps
by as much as four times. The B.S.P. probably only contributed
to the C.P.G.B. a membership of about 2,500; Gallacher's Scottish
group brought in not more than 200; and the 'I.L.P. Left', which
came in after the failure of its efforts to win the whole I.L.P. at its
Easter conference in 1921, could only add between one and two
hundred new members.[3] It was clear that, for a time at least, the
Comintern would have to rely on a very small body of supporters
in Britain.

What manner of men and women were these foundation members of the British Communist Party? Judged as a social group,
their most striking characteristic was their sectionalism. As might
indeed be expected from the story of the party's origins recounted
in the previous chapter, the membership consisted, to a remarkable
degree, of persons of non-English origin. The B.S.P., which had
been the strongest component of the party in England, had always
contained a high proportion of immigrants and exiles from the
Continent, who regarded it as recognisably similar to the Marxist
parties to which they had previously belonged. These elements
had come to the fore in the controversy over foreign policy before
and during the war, and were naturally to be found on the
'internationalist' wing, which caused the defeat of Hyndman in

[1] Lenin, *Selected Works* (1947), ii, 622.
[2] ECCI, *Third Congress Report*, 1921, p. 117.
[3] Bell, *Pioneering Days*, pp. 194f.

1916 and the acceptance of the Bolshevik position in 1918. It was only to be expected that the keenest supporters of the Soviet Union were people like Zelda Kahan (later Mrs Coates) and Theodore Rothstein, whose families had been forced to leave Russia during the pogroms of the Czarist régime. Rothstein, under the pseudonym of 'John Bryan', was the foremost publicist of the Bolsheviks in the B.S.P. press: having never taken British nationality, he was expelled from Britain in 1920 and shortly became the Soviet Union's minister at Teheran.

There was also a large number of Irishmen in the new party. Persons of Irish blood were especially interested in revolutionary activity at this time, when the 'troubles' were at their height in Ireland. The S.L.P. had secured many adherents among the Irish immigrants on Clydeside: indeed, the principal founder of the party had been James Connolly, who was shot for his part in the Dublin Easter Rising of 1916. Arthur MacManus, as we have seen, was the son of a Fenian; Willie Gallacher had an Irish father and a Highland mother; and J. T. Murphy, of Sheffield, also came of mixed parentage, his father being an Irish Catholic and his mother an English Baptist. Further, it is not unreasonable to suppose that the Irish strain was a factor in bringing the party some of its recruits from the professional classes, such as Colonel Malone, the former Coalition M.P.

If we look at the early industrial strength of the party, the 'Celtic fringe' influence in general becomes clear. The Shop Stewards and Workers' Committee movement began to weaken rapidly after the end of the war, with the restoration of free action to the trade unions and the growth of widespread unemployment in the engineering industry. It was merged into the Communist Party under arrangements made shortly after the Second Unity Convention.[1] Only the Clyde Workers' Committee retained a semblance of its earlier importance: it continued to maintain its weekly paper, the *Worker*, which more and more came under Communist control, especially when in 1922 J. R. Campbell became its editor. Even more strikingly sectional was the Communist support among the miners, for it was only in the South

[1] *Communist International*, 16 and 17 (1921), p. 126.

Wales and the Fifeshire coalfields that the seed of the party's gospel
at once struck fertile soil. As early as 1921 the South Wales
Miners Federation passed a resolution in favour of affiliating to
the Red International of Labour Unions which had just been
founded under Moscow control, and Lenin became interested in
the possibility of the South Wales miners forming a mass basis for
the British Communist Party.[1]

It is on sectional lines, therefore, rather than on class lines, that
we can best differentiate the Communists at the time of the formation of their party. A number of people joined, of course, for
no other reason than that they admired the success of the Russian
Bolsheviks in accomplishing their revolution. These were for the
most part young 'intellectuals', who were keenly interested in
foreign affairs and who were at an impressionable age. Some of
them had been Guild Socialists, and their conversion to Communism disrupted the Guild movement. They apparently con-
stituted a majority in the Labour Research Department, an off-
shoot of the Fabian Society, which after two or three years'
manoeuvring they turned into a subsidiary of the Communist
Party.[2] But even in this group the English element was small and
transient. William Mellor, Ellen Wilkinson, Raymond Postgate,
Walton Newbold had all left the party within four or five years;
it was Rajani Palme Dutt, half Indian and half Scandinavian, and
Robin Page Arnot, of Greenock, who were left to carry on, amid
a working-class group of predominantly Celtic origin.

*   *   *

Clearly this very heterogeneous body, with its federal constitution, could as yet have little resemblance to Lenin's conception
of a revolutionary party. The Second Congress of the Comintern
had adopted a series of twenty-one 'theses' – the great bulk of
them drawn up by Lenin – which formed the conditions of
affiliation to the International. In these theses the strict, almost
military nature of the International's discipline was emphasised,

[1] *Lenin on Britain*, p. 272.
[2] For an account of this see R. W. Postgate s article in *Socialist Review*,
April 1934, pp. 6-18.

and it could be justified by the existence of the civil war in which the Bolsheviks were as yet on the defensive. The twelfth thesis declared:

> Parties belonging to the Communist International must be based on the principle of *democratic centralism*. In the present epoch of acute civil war the Communist Party will be able to fulfil its duty only if its organisation is as centralised as possible, if iron discipline prevails, and if the party centre, upheld by the confidence of the party membership, has strength and authority and is equipped with the most comprehensive powers.[1]

This, needless to say, was not the sort of party which had previously existed on the extreme Left in British politics, with its strong nonconformist traditions. But more was to follow: the sixteenth thesis opened:

> All the decisions of the congresses of the Communist International, as well as the decisions of its Executive Committee, are binding on all parties belonging to the Communist International.[2]

Under this provision the British party gave up its political initiative to the International. It remained to be seen, of course, how far this would mean Russian domination: many of the opponents of the party suggested that this was already the case. But it must have been clear to all that since the British party was so small in relation to the other Communist parties, it would have very little say in the decisions which were to determine its own policy. MacManus, its chairman, made no bones about acknowledging this. Speaking at a Rules Conference of the party in Manchester in April 1921, he said that 'The criticism directed against us that we take our dictates from Moscow is not worth replying to'; but he also emphasised that 'The social forces are world-wide. They know no nationality and take no regard of such capitalistic symbols as the Union Jack.'[3]

As for the 'rigid discipline' that the Comintern had enjoined, there was at first little sign of this in the British party. At the Manchester Rules Conference the principle of regional repre-

---

[1] Degras (ed.), *C.I. Documents*, i, 171.   [2] *Ibid.*
[3] *Manchester Guardian*, 25 Apr. 1921.

sentation was again incorporated in the constitution, and the only evidence of discipline – not really a very convincing one, for severe punishment is not necessarily indicative of effective control – was the expulsion of one of the party's most prominent members, Robert Williams the secretary of the National Transport Workers Federation.[1] Williams had been involved in the compromise of the threatened strike of railwaymen and transport workers in support of the miners – the so-called 'Triple Alliance' – and was consequently branded as a 'traitor' to the militant miners, whom the Communist Party were vigorously supporting. In view of the abuse heaped upon his head, it was remarkable that Williams was prepared to support the resolution in favour of the party's affiliation which came up at the Labour Party conference later in the year.[2]

Another case of expulsion which followed later in 1921 indicated the discrepancy between the traditional radical's attitude towards political organisation and that which the Communists were endeavouring to introduce. Sylvia Pankhurst presented a real problem to the party Executive, not only because she retained the ownership and control of a weekly journal, but also because her views were clearly at odds on many questions with those of the party as a whole. In the early summer of 1921, shortly after her release from a six-months' prison sentence, she was interviewed by a sub-committee of the Executive, who, as she reported to her readers,

> ... put it to me that 'as a disciplined member of the party' I should hand the *Workers' Dreadnought* over to the Executive, to stop it, or continue it, and should it continue the paper, to put it to any use or policy it chose, and to place it under the editorship of any person whom it might select: I was not to be consulted, or even informed, till the decision should be made. Thus, with a spice of brutality, the disciplinarians set forth their terms to one who had for eight years maintained a pioneer paper with constant struggle and in face of much persecution.[3]

[1] *Ibid.*; CP, *Constitution and Rules* (1921).
[2] Labour Party *Report*, 1921, p. 164.
[3] *Workers' Dreadnought*, 17 Sept. 1921.

Sylvia Pankhurst refused to obey the sub-committee, and she was later sent an ultimatum to comply, followed by a summons to meet the full Executive in September. In the meantime, she provided some justification for the Executive's attitude by publishing news about the forthcoming formation of a new 'Anti-Parliamentary Communist International'.[1] Her encounter with the Executive was none the less interesting for her arguments against the need for a strictly disciplined party in Britain:

> I told the comrades that if we were before the barricades, if we were in the throes of the revolution, or even somewhere near it, I could approve a rigidity of discipline which is wholly out of place here and now ... that in the weak, young, little-evolved Communist movement of this country discussion is a paramount need, and to stifle it is disastrous ... Comrade MacManus stated that it is he who decides what work shall be allocated to the members ...[2]

There could be no conclusion to this exchange of views except Sylvia Pankhurst's expulsion, and the little British party thus deprived itself of the services of one of its most energetic propagandists.

The party was indeed in grave danger of making sectarianism a substitute for discipline. It was natural that after the rejection of its first attempt to affiliate to the Labour Party in 1920, the party's leaders should let forth their spleen against Ramsay MacDonald when he sought re-election to Parliament at the Woolwich by-election in March 1921.[3] But in August of the same year they went so far as to put up a candidate of their own against a Labour candidate in another by-election at Caerphilly.[4] Yet so far were they from securing the devotion of their own members that in 1922 they had to report to the Comintern a large gap between the total of their adherents and the number of those who had paid their membership fees (sixpence a week). The figures were 5,116 and 2,300 respectively.[5]

[1] *Workers' Dreadnought*, 27 Aug. 1921.   [2] *Ibid.*, 17 Sept. 1921.
[3] Extracts from the CP manifesto saying that 'the Labour candidate stands for Capitalism and all its manifestations' were quoted in Labour Party *Report*, 1921, p. 166.
[4] For a brief but colourful account of the by-election, see J. Jones, *Unfinished Journey*, pp. 202f.   [5] ECCI, *Fourth Congress Report*, 1922, p. 289.

Still, these were the formative years for the Communist parties of all countries outside the Soviet sphere; and it was only in December 1921 that the Comintern drew up a code of procedure for the parties to follow in building their organisations and shaping their tactics.[1] The basis for this code was the series of theses drafted by Lenin and adopted by the Third Congress of the International in July of the same year. At a special conference of the British party in March 1922, a Commission of three members was appointed to translate the Comintern instructions into recommendations for the reshaping of the British party.[2] The members of the Commission were H. W. Inkpin, brother of the party's general secretary; Harry Pollitt, an active young propagandist from the Boilermakers' Union; and Palme Dutt. To assist them in their work they had, as Comintern special representative in Britain, Michael Borodin, a Russian leader who was later to play an important part in China. But Borodin, though concealed under the alias of 'George Brown', was caught by the police later in the year and after serving a short sentence was deported.[3]

The report of the Commission, which ran to eighty pages of close print, was a brilliant translation from the Leninist original, in which we can clearly see the handiwork of Dutt, who had taken Firsts in Classical Moderations and Greats at Balliol. Dutt could not, however, have followed the original so closely in his recommendations if he had not had the support of at least one other member of the commission, and it was important that he gained the confidence of the trade-unionist Pollitt. The mutual trust of these two men, so different in social background, was to have important consequences for the future.

The report began with a scathing indictment of the Social-Democratic party 'branch', in which as a rule a very few members do the work while all the others are inactive and apathetic. By contrast with this, in a Communist Party 'every member would have to be a working member'.[4] At the centre, the report declared,

[1] Degras, *op. cit.*, i, 307-16.
[2] W. Gallacher, *Rolling of the Thunder* (1947), pp. 38f.
[3] *Glasgow Herald*, 30 Aug. 1922; J. T. Murphy, *New Horizons* (1941), pp. 88f, 183f. Murphy acted as Borodin's secretary.
[4] CP, *Report on Organisation* (1922), p. 14.

the old forms of control by individuals must disappear. A Central Committee, comprising a few leading members available for continuous work, must govern the party; this executive should be divided into a Political Bureau and an Organising Bureau. Although a Party Council of larger size, to include representatives from all areas, should exist for occasional consultation, the party must be highly centralised, and the channel of control should run direct from the Central Committee to the District Committees and through the District Committees to the local groups.

At all levels, according to the report, the main activity of the party should be devoted to the trade unions and the workshops. To effect this, two types of organisation were necessary, the 'fraction' and the 'nucleus'. The 'fraction' was a group of Communists on any representative body, such as a trade-union executive or a trades council: the members of the group were to work in close co-ordination, preparing their policy together before the meetings of the larger body, in complete conformity with Communist Party policy and discipline. The 'nucleus' was simply any group of party members who belonged to the same factory or workshop, who were expected to engage in political activity in an organised fashion, also under party discipline.

These were the main recommendations of the report of the Commission, all of them derived from the theses of the Comintern There were certain consequential changes also advocated, such as that the *Communist*, which was not unfairly described as 'a small magazine of miscellaneous articles with a Communist bias',[1] should be transformed into a paper likely to appeal to the factory worker; and that for the purposes of political education, the party should not rely upon the Labour College movement but should build up its own system. Both these proposals hit hard at some of the 'intellectuals' who had been working for the *Communist* or teaching for the Labour Colleges, such as Raymond Postgate and Frank Horrabin. They dropped out of the party, taking with them the Plebs League and the whole Labour College movement, which might have been a valuable ancillary of party propaganda.[2]

[1] CP, *Report on Organisation* (1922), p. 30.
[2] T. Bell, *British Communist Party* (1937), p. 84; Horrabin in *Plebs*, xvii, 287f.

Colonel Malone and Francis Meynell (the printer and book designer, who was the first editor of the *Communist*) seem to have left the party even earlier, probably before the end of 1921.

But the discontent with the proposed changes was not confined to the 'intellectuals'. There was also a good deal of apprehension among the old S.L.P. leaders, who were used to an altogether freer type of organisation. MacManus, Bell and Murphy, at this time the most prominent of the party's leaders in the industrial sphere, all apparently had their doubts.[1] As it was a matter of bringing the British party into line with the other sections of the International, the Executive Committee of the Comintern intervened, and decided on the extraordinary step of inviting the entire Central Committee of the British party to Moscow for consultations.[2] Since, in those days, a return journey to Moscow, with time allowed for business, could hardly be accomplished in less than a month and might take a good deal longer, it was indicative of the importance attached to the consultations on both sides that all of them went, with the exception of Murphy, who had already spent a good many months in Moscow since the revolution, but with the addition of several others not on the Executive. The discussions in Moscow had very much the result that the officials of the International intended: the recalcitrant members were overawed by their revolutionary surroundings and by the great weight of authority of the Russian and other leaders advising them, and they returned to England largely reconciled to the changes. All the same, some of them were still opposed to any speedy reorganisation of the party, and it was in the main the Commission members themselves, in particular Pollitt and Dutt, who had to initiate the measures of 'Bolshevisation' as it was called. Dutt shouldered the burden of editing the weekly organ of the party, now to be known as the *Workers' Weekly* instead of the *Communist*; this was in addition to his responsibility for the more academic *Labour Monthly* of which he was the founder and editor. Pollitt played an increasingly large part in the direction of party work in the industrial sphere. Although by no means in full control, these two men with their complementary qualities were be-

[1] Murphy, *op. cit.*, p. 197.   [2] *Ibid.*, pp. 195f.

ginning to shape the party along the lines approved by the officials of the Comintern in Moscow.

★   ★   ★

The tutelage of the International also assumed paramount importance in the sphere of the party's industrial and political tactics. In 1920 a Red International of Labour Unions (or Profintern, as the Russians called it) had been formed with headquarters in Moscow, and J. T. Murphy, who was in Moscow at the time, was invited by Lenin to join the Provisional Committee and to set on foot the organisation of a 'British Bureau' of the organisation. Travelling illegally at considerable personal risk, he returned to England at the end of the year, carrying a considerable subsidy with which to launch the Bureau.[1] Tom Mann, the veteran pioneer of the 'new unionism', became its President, and it at once established close relations with the Shop Stewards and Workers' Committees. A good deal of sympathy for the Profintern became evident among the Fife and South Wales miners, and with a modicum of support elsewhere a fairly strong delegation could be got together to represent the British Bureau at the foundation Congress of the Profintern in Moscow in 1921.[2]

At the end of that year, however, the British party, and with it, the British Bureau of the Profintern, became involved in the first of those sudden switches of policy which were to become characteristic of Comintern behaviour. A resolution of the Executive Committee of the Comintern instructed its sections to follow a 'united front' tactic. The English party members were specifically ordered to 'begin a vigorous campaign for their acceptance by the Labour Party'.[3] As we have seen, the British Communists had been inclined to accept the rejection of their first attempt to affiliate, and had spent much of their time in attacking the Labour Party. The new tactic also seemed to run

---

[1] Murphy, *op. cit.*, pp. 160-7; information from Mr Murphy. Louis C. Fraina, the American Communist leader, stated that he had received $50,000 from the Comintern in 1920, and had passed on $20,000 of this to Murphy. See Fraina's interrogation by the F.B.I. in 1949, quoted in T. Draper, *Roots of American Communism* (New York, 1957), p. 294.

[2] Murphy, *op. cit.*, pp. 172f.   [3] Degras, *op. cit.*, i, 313.

EXECUTIVE COMMITTEE WITH HEADQUARTER STAFF, 1921

The five men seated are, left to right, Tom Bell, Albert Inkpin, Arthur MacManus, Willie Gallacher, Fred Peet

counter to the idea of setting up a separate Red International of Labour Unions, which naturally conflicted with the International Federation of Trade Unions, the 'Amsterdam International', to which the British T.U.C. belonged. All in all, it is not surprising that the new tactic as Murphy said came as a 'shock' to the British party and at once led to a 'considerable loss of membership'.[1] It was not easy for the British Communists to cast off their sectarian tradition. Tommy Jackson, one of their working-class theoreticians, hardly improved matters at the Party Policy Congress in March 1922 when he paraphrased Lenin and declared of the Labour Party leaders: 'I would take them by the hand as a preliminary to taking them by the throat.'[2]

However, the Moscow line was as usual accepted; and it was decided to withdraw the party's prospective candidates from any constituencies where Labour candidates had already been adopted. The arrangement was facilitated by the fact that, owing to the looseness of the Labour Party constitution, it was still possible for an open Communist to belong to a Labour Party branch, and indeed to be adopted as an official Labour candidate. Thus when a General Election took place in November 1922, two out of seven Communist candidates were elected, one of them having stood as an official Labour candidate and the other as a Communist but without Labour opposition. The former was Shapurji Saklatvala, a Bombay Parsee who won Battersea North; the latter was Walton Newbold, who was elected for Motherwell. Unfortunately for the Communists, the Labour Party did not allow this situation to continue: it rejected by large majorities the Communist Party's annual applications for affiliation; and in 1924 it decided that members of the C.P.G.B. were not eligible for endorsement as Labour candidates.[3]

Meanwhile in the industrial sphere the party made only very slow progress. The British Bureau of the Profintern seemed merely to duplicate the party's own organisation; and the task of forming party 'nuclei' was greatly hindered by the trade depression. Too many of the party's members were unemployed, and those who

[1] ECCI, *Fourth Congress Report*, p. 61. [2] *Communist*, 25 Mar. 1922.
[3] Labour Party *Report*, 1924, pp. 123-31.

c

were still in jobs were acutely aware of the dangers of victimisation. The only promising development was that the party obtained a strong grip on the National Unemployed Workers' Committee Movement. This body, formed in 1921, was run by a tough young Communist called Wal Hannington who was an engineer's toolmaker. The situation, as he later rather disingenuously expressed it, was that

> The National Conference of the Unemployed in 1921 did not consist of a majority of Communist Party members, but the quality of the party leadership was acknowledged by the delegates electing party members as officials of the National Movement.[1]

The problems of the British Bureau of the Profintern were not ignored in Moscow, and its affairs were thoroughly discussed when the British party Executive visited the Russian capital early in 1923. It was decided that the object of the British Bureau was

> ... not to organise independent revolutionary unions or to split the revolutionary elements away from the existing organisations affiliated to the T.U.C. and through it to the Amsterdam International, but to convert the revolutionary minorities existing in the various industries, into revolutionary majorities. Hence the British Bureau is not an organisation of unions but only of revolutionary minorities of unions.[2]

This decision was a realistic one, for in Britain there was no tradition of 'dual unionism' as existed in some other countries, and any attempt to found unions in rivalry with those already in existence would be regarded as the greatest of sins. Indeed it was specifically decided that

> Where separate districts break away from the main body and form independent revolutionary unions, the Bureau does its utmost to liquidate the split and get the seceded group to return to its parent organisation.[3]

To effect this industrial policy, which was in line with the

---

[1] *WNV*, xxx, 321.
[2] See ch. xiv of RILU, 'International Labour Movement 1923-4', typescript report of executive bureau to Third Congress delegates. Copy in T.U.C. Library.   [3] *Ibid.*

general tactic of the 'united front', the personnel of the Bureau was changed, and Gallacher was instructed to take charge and to organise a national conference to launch the movement under the new and more innocuous name of 'Minority Movement'.[1] Lavish subsidies were provided, and the movement was equipped with a host of journals – the monthly *All Power*, the weekly *Worker* (taken over from the waning Glasgow Workers' Committee), and, for particular industries, the fortnightly *Mine Worker*, the *International Seaman*, and the *International Metal Workers' Bulletin*.[2] The greatest success was registered with the miners, who were persuaded to elect A. J. Cook, the Minority Movement candidate, as their general secretary when Frank Hodges retired. The central direction, however, was still very weak: no effective 'fraction' work was done at the T.U.C. meetings before 1924, and the militant Fife miners, instead of obeying the 'united front' tactic, insisted on seceding from the Scottish Mineworkers' Union to form a separate body, their leaders simultaneously leaving the Communist Party.[3] Even the national conference to inaugurate the Minority Movement could not be arranged before the summer of 1924 – a delay which was the subject of an exchange of rebukes between the Profintern 'troika' in Moscow (Lozovsky, Kalnin and Nin, who were in charge of the Secretariat) and Gallacher in London.[4] When the national conference took place, Pollitt took over the management of the Minority Movement from Gallacher under a reshuffle which, it is hardly necessary to add, had been arranged before the conference met.[5]

*   *   *

Throughout these early years the party had begun to grow accustomed to the bitter hostility of public opinion and the close surveillance of the police. The fact that the British Communists so completely identified themselves with the Russian Bolsheviks, and took subsidies from them, was the main reason for this. Like

[1] *Ibid.*, ch. xv.
[2] See correspondence with Lozovsky, *Parliamentary Papers*, 1926, xxiii, 653f.
[3] RILU, *op. cit.*, ch. xii.
[4] Gallacher, *Rolling of the Thunder*, p. 48.
[5] *Ibid.*, p. 47; *National Minority Conference Report* (1924).

the Roman Catholic minority of the Elizabethan age, the Communists were feared not only for their own revolutionary potential but also because they seemed to be the agents of a hostile foreign power. Scotland Yard was on the lookout for Comintern agents of foreign nationality, who could immediately be deported under existing legislation. The police had their informers among the members of the party,[1] and the Bolshevik agents who came on permanent or temporary mission from the Comintern headquarters had to keep their identity secret even from their fellow-Communists. Thus Borodin, as we have seen, was known to the British party as 'George Brown', and D. Petrovsky, who in 1924 assumed the position of permanent representative of the Executive Committee of the Comintern in Britain – in effect, Comintern ambassador – was concealed under the pseudonym of 'A. J. Bennet'.[2]

The British members of the party were also kept under close surveillance, although they could not be deported. In 1921 Albert Inkpin, the general secretary, was arrested and sentenced to six months' hard labour – not so much for his own sins as for those of the International in general. His 'crime' was to have published in Britain a translated edition of the theses of the Comintern.[3] Officers of Scotland Yard were constantly on the watch at party meetings, noting down the speeches made with a view to possible prosecution. To obtain evidence the police sometimes adopted undignified and possibly illegal stratagems: in April 1924, for instance, a couple of plain clothes officers were discovered hiding under the stage of the Rehearsal Theatre, Bedford Street, where the party Executive was due to hold a meeting. The Communists seized the officers' notebooks and handed the officers themselves

[1] For the fate of Harry Johnstone, a police informer in the N.U.W.M., see *Parl. Deb.*, ser. 5, ccix, 1563f; W. Hannington, *Unemployed Struggles 1919-36* (1936), pp. 146-53; L. Paul, *Angry Young Man* (1951), pp. 92-102.
[2] Petrovsky was on duty in England in 1924, according to Ruth Fischer, *Stalin and German Communism* (1948), p. 400. He published two pamphlets in Britain under his pseudonym, *The General Council and the General Strike* (1926) and *War: the Communist International's Position* (1927). For a tribute to his work from the British party see *Inprecorr*, viii, 1744.
[3] *The Times*, 29 June 1921.

over to the nearest police constable in uniform, who, not re-
cognising them, promptly took them in charge.[1]

By 1924 a Labour Government had come to power, and the
Communists had reason to hope that the stringency of police
supervision of their activities would be relaxed. Many of the
leaders of the Labour Party, including Ramsay MacDonald himself, were inclined to accept Frank Hodges' description of them
(at the 1922 Labour Party Conference) as 'intellectual slaves of
Moscow . . . taking orders from the Asiatic mind'.[2] There was
however a good deal of sympathy for the party in its difficulties
with the police, at least among the Labour back-benchers; and,
so far as Russia itself was concerned, the official Labour policy was
to seek an early *rapprochement*. At the same time, the Labour Party
had no parliamentary majority, and the government survived
only on the goodwill of the Liberals. The Conservative leaders
were constantly on the look-out for any tendency on the part of
ministers to be 'soft' towards the Communists: this was an issue,
they realised, on which they could expect to obtain Liberal support
against the government. Consequently, although MacDonald and
his colleagues managed to make a trade agreement with the
Soviet Union, their downfall was due to a supposed leniency
towards an offending member of the Communist Party.

In July 1924 the *Workers' Weekly*, the official journal of the
party, published a 'Don't Shoot' appeal to the troops rather
similar to that for which Tom Mann and others were imprisoned
in 1911.[3] The article was the culmination of an anti-war campaign
which was carried out on the instructions of the Comintern. The
editor of the *Workers' Weekly* was no longer Dutt, who had
collapsed under the strain of all his party responsibilities and,
owing to chronic illness, became an invalid for several years. His
successor on the paper was J. R. Campbell, who was accordingly
charged with incitement to mutiny. On investigation of the case,
however, the Attorney-General, Sir Patrick Hastings, decided to
withdraw the prosecution. The Conservatives at once raised a

[1] *Parl. Deb.*, ser. 5, clxxii, 928; *Workers' Weekly*, 18 Apr. 1924; police
officer's evidence in Communist trial, *The Times*, 19 Nov. 1925.
[2] Labour Party *Report*, 1922, p. 198.   [3] *Workers' Weekly*, 25 July 1924.

great outcry, arguing that this decision was the result of political bias in favour of a Communist. The matter was thoroughly debated when the Commons met at the end of September. The Attorney-General maintained that he had withdrawn the prosecution only because he had discovered that Campbell was a man of excellent character – unlike so many of the Communist leaders, he had served in the forces during the war, had been decorated for gallantry and was permanently disabled by wounds – and that moreover he was probably not directly responsible for the article, being only the temporary editor and not a member of the governing committee of the party, the Politburo.[1]

Whether or not these were in fact the true reasons for the withdrawal of the prosecution, it was a mistake to say that Campbell was not a member of the Politburo, as the Conservatives at once pointed out; and the Communists themselves were reported to be claiming the withdrawal of the prosecution as 'a victory for the rank and file'. The Liberal Party proposed that a Select Committee of the House should be appointed to look into the matter and report; Ramsay MacDonald could have accepted this as a compromise, but he refused to do so, and in effect challenged the Liberals to withdraw or bring down the government. The Liberals did not withdraw, and their proposal was carried by a united vote of Liberals and Conservatives; whereupon MacDonald secured a dissolution of Parliament.

The General Election, which took place on 29th October, was powerfully affected by yet another sensation affecting the Communist Party. This was the famous 'Zinoviev letter', a copy of which came into the hands of the *Daily Mail* in time for publication four days before election day. The letter, which purported to be a message from Zinoviev, the general secretary of the Communist International, to the leaders of the British party, contained instructions for the organisation of 'Communist cells' in the army and navy, in order to paralyse British military operations in the event of war. A special air of authenticity was given to the document by the Foreign Office, which sought to anticipate the *Daily Mail* by hastily publishing the letter officially, together

[1] *Parl. Deb.*, ser. 5, clxxvii, 8-10.

with a note of protest to the Soviet Government.[1] Ramsay
MacDonald, who was on a campaign tour at the time, was unable
to confirm or deny the letter's authenticity, and the Conservative
press made considerable capital out of the affair for election purposes. In the upshot, the Conservatives secured an easy victory
at the polls, largely at the expense of the Liberals; and the representation of the Labour Party sank from 193 to 151. The
Communists, who had had no members in the 1923-4 House,
were lucky to secure the return of one member – Saklatvala, who
won back his seat at Battersea North.

The authenticity of the 'Zinoviev letter' remains disputed to
this day.[2] There can be no doubt that the leaders of the International were fully capable of expressing the sentiments that it
contained. But there are strong reasons for considering it a forgery.
The 'military section of the British Communist Party', to which
it referred, does not seem to have had any existence. There were
unusual features about its form, which were at once pointed out
by C.P.G.B. spokesmen: it was not usual, for instance, for the
Communist International to call itself the 'Third International',
or for the local groups of one of its sections to be known at this
time as 'cells'. Further, the way in which the Foreign Office and
the *Daily Mail* obtained copies of the letter was never satisfac-
torily cleared up, and there is reason to connect it with *émigré*
Russian circles. Finally, on the test of *cui bono?* it is clear that the
Conservative Party stood to gain considerably from an extension
of the 'Red scare' which had produced the Campbell case. Although none of the revolutionary methods advocated in the letter
could be regarded as alien to Comintern practice, the inclusion of
such phrases as 'the future directors of the British Red Army' was
almost too good to be true for the purposes of anti-Communist
propaganda.

By the end of 1924, therefore, the British Communist Party
could claim to have had some influence on the course of national
history. But this was by courtesy of the Conservatives and their

[1] *The Times*, 25 Oct. 1924.
[2] For a recent discussion of the subject, see R. W. Lyman, *First Labour
Government, 1924* (1957), esp. pp. 286-9.

press, and not through any positive influence of its own. Its membership, though slowly rising, was still less than 5,000, and this was in spite of lavish funds received from Moscow, which in the course of the year allocated £5,000 for the direct needs of the party, apart from what was sent for the Minority Movement.[1] The 'slow development of the British party', which had caused concern in Moscow in 1922 and 1923, still showed no signs of acceleration: the only hope for the immediate future lay in the disappointment and frustration felt by the Labour rank and file.

[1] ECCI, *C.I. between Fifth and Sixth World Congresses* (1928), p. 30; *Parliamentary Papers*, 1926, xxiii, 661.

CHAPTER III

'STALINISATION', 1924-9

AFTER the 1924 General Election the militancy of the Labour movement had no outlet save in the industrial sphere. The Conservatives had a considerable clear majority in Parliament over both the Labour and Liberal Parties combined, and for the time being Baldwin's government seemed secure. The leaders of the Labour Party not unnaturally felt aggrieved with the Communists who had been so largely, if indirectly, responsible for their downfall. It had already been decided that Communists were no longer eligible as Labour Party candidates for Parliament, but some confusion arose over a decision of the 1924 conference that they should be altogether ineligible in future as members of the party, for this infringed the freedom of the trade unions in what was after all a federal organisation of industrial as well as political bodies. A few Communists were in fact delegated to attend the 1925 Labour Party Conference in defiance of this decision. To meet the situation the Labour Party Executive produced a recommendation that members of the Communist Party should be formally excluded only from the individual sections of the affiliated local Labour Parties. This compromise left the trade unions free to act as they thought fit, while at the same time considerably weakening in general the Communist foothold inside the Labour Party. The 1925 Labour Party Conference accepted the recommendation by a majority of about nine to one.[1]

But if they received a severe setback at the Labour Party Conference in that year, the Communists could find consolation in their success at the Trades Union Congress. By this time the Minority Movement was becoming better organised: as we have seen, its members had already been heartened by the election of A. J. Cook as successor to Frank Hodges in the key post of

[1] Labour Party *Report*, 1925, pp. 181-7.

secretary of the Miners Federation. Ten Communists were among the over seven hundred delegates to the 1925 T.U.C., and this tiny minority – the 'Fraction of Ten' as it was known[1] – was so well organised before and during the Congress, and, more important, the temper of the delegates as a whole was so militant, that many of the resolutions to which the Communist Party attached most urgency were carried. The long and bitter conflict in the coal industry, which had aroused widespread sympathy for the miners' situation among the workers of other trades, was largely responsible for this general stiffening of attitude at the T.U.C. The General Council had already gone so far as to establish close relations with the Russian trade unions by means of the Anglo-Russian Joint Council, a committee set up for purposes of mutual consultation and assistance, and with the further object of effecting a reconciliation between the Profintern and the 'Amsterdam International' to which the T.U.C. was affiliated.

From this point onwards, the threat of a General Strike dominated British politics, and the Conservative Government began to prepare for the conflict. A body called the Organisation for the Maintenance of Supplies was set up to make plans for the operation of essential services in an emergency; and, true to its belief in the magnitude of the Communist threat, the Government set on foot a prosecution of twelve leading Communists for sedition under the Mutiny Act of 1797. At the same time the Communist headquarters in King Street, Covent Garden, and the offices of the Minority Movement in Great Ormond Street were raided for the acquisition of evidence. On the whole, this prosecution was a mistake, for although all the accused were found guilty and sent to prison for terms of either six months or a year, the case had provided them with a golden opportunity for the advertisement of their views, while counsel for the Crown made rather heavy weather of proving the seditious character of Marxist-Leninism – as distinct, for instance, from the doctrines of the Second International.[2] At the same time, the evidence produced at the trial,

[1] See CP Agit-Prop report to C.I. Agit-Prop, 29 Aug. 1925, *Parliamentary Papers*, 1926, xxiii, 673.
[2] See, e.g., report of the case in *The Times*, 29 Oct. 1925.

subsequently published as a Blue Book, provided useful information for the leaders of the Labour Party and the trade unions
as to the essential features of the Comintern plan for winning
control of the British working class movement.[1]

Meanwhile, the crisis in the coalfields had only been postponed
by the appointment in 1925 of the Samuel Commission, which
sat through the winter and presented its findings in March.
Opposing nationalisation of the mines, and faced with a serious
slump in British coal exports, the Commission could only recom-
mend a reduction in miners' wages; consequently, the Mineworkers Federation, which but a few years before had been
promised the nationalisation of the industry, considered the report
quite unacceptable. The General Council of the T.U.C. now
swung its weight behind the strikers, and threatened a General
Strike unless concessions were made. The Government refused to
bow to the threat, and the strike, for which virtually no detailed
preparations had been made on the trade union side before 27th
April, began on 4th May, 1926.

This is not the place to tell the story of the nine days that
followed – nine days that fortunately have proved unique in
British history. Although the workers called out on strike dis-
played a remarkable degree of solidarity, few serious disturbances
occurred, and the whole affair proved conclusively that in spite
of their sense of grievance the workers had no desire to resort to
revolutionary action or to challenge the forces of law and order.
Their leaders were even more cautious: after Sir John Simon had
solemnly declared the strike illegal, they leapt at the slightest hint
of compromise to call the strike off, and the men were sent back
to work without any official concessions having been made to
meet the claims of the miners. Indeed, the miners remained on
strike for six months afterwards, being eventually beaten into
submission by sheer hunger.

Although the Communist Party itself was taken by surprise
when the strike began,[2] it naturally assumed an attitude of the

[1] 'Communist Papers', *Parliamentary Papers*, 1926, xxiii, 585-743.
[2] J. T. Murphy, *Political Meaning of the Great Strike* (1926), p. 80. The best
account of the strike is still W. H. Crook, *General Strike* (Chapel Hill, N.C.,

keenest militancy, hampered though it was by having its most prominent leaders still in prison. Detailed instructions for the operation of 'fractions' on Trades Councils and Councils of Action were sent out from King Street, and these were followed by frequent 'leads' as the situation altered.[1] An abnormally high proportion of Communists were arrested in the course of the nine days: this was partly, no doubt, because the police hoped to cripple the activities of party members, but principally because the Communists enjoyed the martyrdom of arrest and imprisonment for the cause, whereas the average worker was only interested on escaping the attentions of the police if he could honourably do so. On the last day of the strike, 12th May, the Politburo of the C.P.G.B. issued a 'lead' to the workers against a resumption of work[2]; and thereafter the party constantly denounced the members of the T.U.C. General Council for their 'betrayal' of the miners.

Naturally, Communist militancy along these lines brought the party a certain popularity among the more embittered sections of the working class, and particularly among the miners, who welcomed the party's continued support after the end of the General Strike. Communist Party membership suddenly shot up: it had reached 6,000 before the strike, but by October 1926 it had risen to 10,730, the great majority of the new recruits being miners.[3] It was no wonder that Stalin could at the time speak of the C.P.G.B. as being 'one of the best sections' of the Comintern, and could say that its attitude to the strike had been 'perfectly correct'.[4] Unfortunately for the British Communist leaders, however, their popularity did not last long: in November, when the miners' strike finally collapsed, the bankruptcy of a policy of sheer militancy became obvious. The new recruits that the party had made began to leave almost as quickly as they had joined: and by October 1927 the total membership was down to 7,377, and still falling rapidly.[5]

*   *   *

1931), who quotes this passage. But see also J. Symons, *General Strike* (1957).
[1] CP, *Eighth Congress Report* 1926, p. 6.   [2] *Ibid.*, p. 9.
[3] ECCI, *C.I. between Fifth and Sixth World Congresses*, p. 30; CP, *Congress Report* 1926, p. 39.   [4] *Inprecorr*, vi, 816.   [5] *Ibid.*, vii, 1288f.

The decline of the Communist Party after the end of the miners' strike was also due to a natural reaction against its highly mechanical methods of seeking influence in the working-class movement. The right-wing leaders of both the Labour Party and the T.U.C. were not slow to reveal details of these methods. Thus at the beginning of July 1926 a Labour Party circular was published quoting from the Government Blue Book of Communist documents, which had just appeared, to show how the 'fraction' and 'nucleus' operated in working-class organisations, with complete subordination of the interests of the organisations concerned to those of the Communist Party. To this circular was attached a copy of an instruction issued by the London District of the C.P.G.B. only a week previously, giving detailed orders for Communist activity on the London Trades Council and in the Labour Party itself.[1]

This type of activity, as we have seen, was based on the tactics laid down by Lenin in 1921 for the operation of Communist parties. Owing complete devotion to their own centralised leadership, it was impossible for Communists to collaborate with non-Communists on a basis of free and equal loyalty to some other principle or institution. Nevertheless, especially in the period of the 'united front', the Communists were prepared to work inside organisations which they had not themselves created, but whose aims or tactics for the time being suited their purposes. It was normally their intention, however, to make such organisations subordinate to the party as soon as possible – an object which could best be served by the creation of a Communist 'fraction' consisting of all the party members of each organisation concerned. Once it had fallen into effective party control, each body could be made to serve any of a number of party purposes: it could act as a means of Communist propaganda among unsuspecting persons, as an agency of recruitment to the party, and if necessary – supposing the party were declared illegal – as a 'cover' for the existence of the party itself.

At first, the most important body in a filial relationship to the Comintern was a genuine creation of its own, the Profintern or

[1] Labour Party *Report*, 1926, pp. 319f.

Red International of Labour Unions, the British section of which, as we have seen, was known from 1923 as the Minority Movement. But the system was soon extended. In 1921 Willi Münzenburg, a German Communist leader, founded the Workers International Relief, which raised contributions for economic assistance to the Soviet Union in its early stages of famine and reconstruction.[1] It was discovered before long that this body could serve many purposes of propaganda and agitation for the party. A similar organisation, founded in the following year, was the International Red Aid, or as it became known in Britain, the International Class War Prisoners Aid. This was used to raise funds for strikers or other victims of 'class warfare' in any country.[2]

The principal aim of all these bodies was indicated most clearly by Kuusinen, the Finnish Communist who was prominent in the Comintern Secretariat. In 1926 he instructed all the sections of the International to build up what he described as a 'whole solar system' of organisations around itself, controlled by the party but nominally independent, each of them to serve as a 'bridge to the masses', for the purpose of developing the influence of the party.[3] The control was of course essential: and as the secretary of the International Red Aid in Moscow put it in 1925, 'With the centre under party control there is little if any danger of political mistakes'[4] – that is, of the organisation developing a policy which at any point ran counter to that of the party.

The role of the non-Communist 'masses' in these bodies was not conceived of in very flattering terms. The Communist 'fraction' in each case was to be the driving force, and the mass membership was to be simply the driven wheel at the end of a 'transmission belt' of power operated by the Communists. The mechanical analogy was one first used by Lenin[5]: it implied, on

[1] See W. Münzenberg, *Fünf Jahre Internationale Arbeiterhilfe* (Berlin, 1926); F. Adler in *Labour Magazine* iii (1924), 350f. Adler quotes Münzenberg's remark at a meeting of the W.I.R. that its branches were 'Innocents' Clubs'.

[2] The incidental advantages are frankly canvassed in the Moscow secretary's letter to the CP, 14 Sept. 1925, *Parliamentary Papers* 1926, xxiii, 715.

[3] *Inprecorr*, vi, 429.

[4] To CP, 14 Sept. 1925, *Parliamentary Papers*, 1926, xxiii, 716.

[5] Lenin, 'Role and function of the trade unions under N.E.P.', *Selected*

the one hand, a high degree of efficiency and discipline on the part
of the Communists, and on the other hand, an attitude of docility
and political apathy among the non-Communist 'masses', whose
role indeed resembled that of the 'dead souls' of Gogol. The
appropriate qualities were not always present, either among the
Communists or among the non-Communist members of the
British 'satellite' bodies in this period. Sometimes the Communists running the organisation would become interested in it
for its own sake, and consequently refuse to obey the party discipline whenever this seemed to run counter to their own view
of the organisation's welfare. This was especially likely to happen
in trade-union work: and the attitude of the Fife miners to the
current 'line' was a case in point. Sometimes the non-Communists
turned out to be capable of breaking off segments of the organisation as soon as they found it to be Communist-dominated – as
occurred more than once in the Unemployed Workers' Committee Movement[1] – though they could rarely capture or recap-
ture the whole organisation, for a Communist 'fraction' once in
control was almost irremovable. Of course, if the party itself were
to decide, usually owing to a change of the existing 'line', that
one of its 'satellite' bodies was of no further use, it would itself
destroy the body concerned with brutal speed, often to the stupe-
faction of the more gullible non-Communists who had been its
members. This was easy for the Communists to do because, in
any body that they controlled, it was customary for them to have
secured all or most of the executive posts for members of the
party, although the honorary positions would be occupied by an
array of non-Communist 'figurehead' nominees for display
purposes.

*   *   *

With this pattern of Communist technique in mind, it is interesting to examine in a little more detail the history of two of the

Works (1947), ii, 766. For a diagram illustrating the 'transmission belts' in
operation, see ECCI, Der Organisatorische Aufbau der Kommunistischen Partei
(Hamburg, 1925), p. 168.
[1] See, e.g., Workers' Dreadnought, 1 Sept. 1923.

bodies under the control of the British party. One of these, the National Left Wing Movement, was founded shortly after the 1925 Labour Party Conference, and had among its objects the reversal of the decisions excluding Communists from the constituency parties. It has often been claimed, and not only by Communists, that this body was able to mobilise a considerable degree of support which might almost entitle it to be regarded as a 'mass movement'. It had a weekly newspaper, the *Sunday Worker*, which lasted for several years in the nineteen-twenties, and its annual conference reports claimed the affiliation of organisations whose aggregate membership ran into six figures. Yet to those who took the trouble to examine the details of the organisation, there was never any doubt that it was from the start completely under Communist control. In the first place, the 'National Left Wing' did not initiate the *Sunday Worker*, but rather the other way about: the paper was founded in 1924, and its staff sponsored the first conference of the National Left Wing in December 1925.[1] Although the paper claimed to be the organ of a broad left-wing movement, its principal shareholders were Communists; its editors – first William Paul, then Walter Holmes – were members of the party; and its serious financial deficit was met by funds supplied by the Comintern – £4,000 in 1925 alone, for instance, and probably equally large sums in subsequent years.[2]

There is no doubt, however, that the National Left Wing caused a certain degree of embarrassment to the leaders of the Labour Party. It acted as a focus of attachment for the rebellious local Labour Parties which, whether owing to Communist control or not, refused to operate the decisions of the 1925 Conference. By the summer of 1927, the Labour Party Executive had had to disaffiliate altogether twenty-three local Labour Parties, fifteen of them in the London area, which had refused to conform to the majority decisions.[3] But once the disaffiliation took place the popular support for the rebel parties, if it had ever existed, soon disappeared. This was shown, for instance, by the failure of the

---

[1] See leader in *Sunday Worker*, 13 Dec. 1925.
[2] CP letter to 'Bennet', autumn 1925, *Parliamentary Papers*, 1926, xxiii, 666.
[3] Labour Party *Report*, 1926, p. 19 and 1927, p. 15.

DEFENDANTS IN THE COMMUNIST TRIAL, 1925

Left to right (front): T. A. Jackson, J. T. Murphy, Harry Pollitt, William Rust, Tom Wintringham, J. R. Campbell, Arthur MacManus, Wal Hannington, Tom Bell, Willie Gallacher

See page 34

National Left Wing in the 1928 L.C.C. elections, when out of
twenty-two candidates not one was returned.[1] Finally, when in
1929 the Communist Party decided, owing to a change of Comintern policy, to suppress the movement and to close down the
Sunday Worker, these decisions took immediate effect in spite of
the protests of various non-Communist Left Wingers, for the
secretary of the National Left Wing, R. E. Bond, and a majority
of his committee were in fact members of the C.P.G.B.[2]

Another example of a 'satellite' organisation of the British
Communist Party, though under very different circumstances, is
provided by the Workers and Peasants Party of India. By Comintern edict, the task of building up Communist propaganda
throughout the British Empire was entrusted to the British party
– a decision that was not at all to the taste of the only prominent
Indian Communist of the early years, M. N. Roy, who said that
it 'smacked of imperialism'.[3] Under constant pressure from
Moscow to act upon this responsibility, the British party formed
a 'Colonial Department', and began to send out emissaries to
develop activities in selected areas. James Crossley, a Manchester
Communist, was sent to Egypt in 1925, and a series of agents was
despatched to India – Percy Glading in 1925, George Allison and
Philip Spratt in 1926, and Ben Bradley in 1927.[4] Spratt, a young
Cambridge graduate, was briefed on his tasks by Petrovsky, the
Comintern agent in Britain, and by Clemens Dutt, the brother of
Palme Dutt, on behalf of the Colonial Department of the British
party.[5] Since it was illegal to belong to the Communist Party in
India, he was to encourage the few Indian Communists to get together in a 'cover' organisation, to be known as the Workers and
Peasants Party of India. He was also to act as a correspondent
between the British and Indian Communists, and for this purpose
he was provided with ciphers and invisible ink. For further dis-
guise he made use on occasion of a rather obvious system of

[1] *Sunday Worker*, 11 Mar. 1928.   [2] *Ibid.*, 10 Mar. 1929.
[3] R. W. Robson's report of Amsterdam Colonial Conference, July 1925,
Parliamentary Papers, 1926, xxiii, 689.
[4] *Parliamentary Papers*, 1926, xxiii, 679ff; M. R. Masani, *Communist Party
of India* (1954), pp. 25f.
[5] P. Spratt, *Blowing Up India* (Calcutta, 1955), pp. 29f.

D

circumlocution, by pretending to be a missionary writing home to colleagues in the home country: he would start off his letters to Dutt 'Dear Brother in God', and then after various references to the 'Y.M.C.A.' (Communist Party) or 'Methodists' (Workers and Peasants Party) would sign himself 'Father Ambrose'. On one occasion, being in need of a supply of Marxist literature, he wrote to England asking for 'a miscellaneous collection of the more recent works of piety and devotion'.

Unfortunately for Spratt, his activities were being closely watched by the police, who had had a very good idea of the activities of the C.P.G.B. in India ever since the trial of the British party's leaders in 1925. The invisible ink with which he had been supplied in London also failed to work properly, and his letters could easily be read on interception. The result was that the Government of India was able in 1929 to arrest all the leading Communists in India, whether Indian or British, and to stage a special conspiracy trial – the Meerut Conspiracy Case, which dragged on for four years and finally ended in 1933.[1]

By the time of his arrest Spratt and his associates had founded several branches of the Workers and Peasants Party in different parts of India, and the plan was that the organisation should be affiliated, not directly to the Comintern or to the British party, but to the League Against Imperialism, another of the creations of the versatile Willi Münzenburg, which had headquarters in Berlin and sections in all the leading countries.[2] It had been intended that communications and financial assistance should pass through this channel, for the purpose of the secret development of the Indian Communist Party. As it turned out, however, the party was broken up by the Meerut arrests; the Comintern adopted the device of using American citizens to try to put it on its feet again, though with little success[3]; and the British party limited itself to agitation and propaganda among Indian students in Britain, some of whom proved to be valuable recruits. As M. R.

[1] See *Meerut Conspiracy Case Judgment* (Simla, 1932-3) for a fascinating survey of the evidence.

[2] *Ibid.*, p. 106; Labour and Socialist International *Report*, 1928, ii, 47.

[3] Masani, *op. cit.*, pp. 45f.

Masani, the historian of the Indian Communist Party, rather sourly remarks, 'The aristocracy of the Communist Party, as of other parties in India, is today (1954) drafted to a certain extent from the class of people whose parents could afford an expensive foreign education.'[1]

*   *   *

In the process of proliferating its 'satellite' organisations at the behest of Moscow, the British Communist Party became even more dependent on the International for financial assistance. The party sought to keep secret both the extent of its receipts in this way, and also the route by which the money came: but in 1928 Scotland Yard was able to detect the transfer of more than one five-figure sum through the Moscow Narodny Bank in London.[2] At the same time the party also became closely interlocked with the agencies of the Soviet Government itself. 'Arcos', which was the Russian trading mission in London, may or may not have been a channel for Soviet espionage, as the British Government claimed in 1927 when it authorised the searching of its premises: it certainly employed a considerable number of British citizens – in fact, over two hundred – many of whom were members of the party.[3] The employees of 'Arcos' and other Soviet agencies in Britain formed a trade union, which was known as 'Mestkom', and had as its secretary Alexander Squair, a London Communist.[4] British party members were also at first recruited to man Soviet ships, but this practice was found to have its disadvantages: one Soviet official maintained that the men recruited in this way were 'completely unaccustomed to work', owing to long periods of unemployment, and moreover 'assume that their membership of the British Communist Party will guarantee their wages and will entitle them to do no work at all'.[5]

[1] *Ibid.*, p. 47.
[2] See 'Russian Banks and Communist Funds', *Parliamentary Papers*, 1928, xii, 275-332.
[3] *Parl. Deb.*, ser. 5, ccviii, 862.
[4] *Ibid.*, ccxviii, 640; *Parliamentary Papers*, 1928, xii, 312.
[5] 'Hostile Activities of the Soviet Government and Third International', *Parliamentary Papers*, 1927, xxvi, 327-58; esp. p. 345.

'Arcos' was disbanded, on the order of the British Government, in 1927; and presumably the Russian mercantile marine began to depend less and less upon the recruitment of sailors in Britain. Nevertheless, the ties between the Soviet Union and the British party increased in many other ways. There were always the British representatives on the Presidium of the International, and the assistants in the Comintern and Profintern Secretariats, as well as the delegations to the innumerable congresses and 'plenums'[1]; there were British Communists who worked in Soviet factories, or in research institutions such as the Marx-Engels Institute, or who were in training at the Lenin School in Moscow, where from 1926 onwards promising members of all sections of the Comintern attended courses in the art of Communist leadership.[2] Such a high degree of association with the Russian Communists and with the Moscow apparatus would have made it almost impossible for the tiny British party ever to have asserted its independence, even had it wanted to. This was the more serious, because by the later nineteen-twenties it was becoming increasingly clear that the Comintern itself was entirely at the mercy of the Russian leaders.

Theoretically, of course, the Communist Party of the Soviet Union was merely one of the member parties of the Comintern, and had no control over it. In practice, however, the situation was very different. There was, first of all, the fact that the apparatus of the Comintern was in Moscow, and its congresses were always held there. Then, further, the Comintern drew the bulk of its finances by *per capita* payments from the members of Communist Parties, and as over half the total world membership of the Communist Parties was in the Soviet Union, this gave the Russian party a virtual financial stranglehold on the Comintern. To suppose that the Russian leaders did not take advantage of this

[1] These years saw the development of the RILU 'International Propaganda Committees', one for each industry. Britain was represented on fifteen of these in 1927. See RILU, 'Work of the Adherents of RILU in the International Federations', mimeographed report for delegates to Fourth RILU Congress, Moscow, 1928, p. 1. Copy in author's possession.

[2] Selection of entrants for the first course at the Lenin School is discussed in ECCI Agit-Prop to CP, 23 June 1925, *Parliamentary Papers*, 1926, xxiii, 623.

situation would be flagrantly un-Marxist.[1] Yet they wished, at least in the earlier years, to preserve the appearances of independence for the Comintern. Unfortunately, however, it rapidly became clear that the factional struggles inside the Russian party could not be isolated from the Comintern. 'Tendencies' which had developed inside the Soviet Union, and which were harshly suppressed – the opposition of Trotsky and then that of Zinoviev and Bukharin – were suspected in the parties of the other countries. If any party attempted to follow its own path, claiming that the objective situation inside the country it represented was different, it had against it the combined weight of the Russian leaders and the delegates from other countries, who in matters not affecting themselves directly were inclined to side with the Russians.

It was undoubtedly awkward, from the point of view of the Comintern Secretariat, that the leadership of the British party seemed to be firmly in the hands of a united caucus, rather than in dispute by two or three factions, sufficiently well-balanced against each other to make the slightest Moscow influence decisive. The C.P.G.B., indeed, seemed largely indifferent to the bitter quarrels which counted for so much among the continental Leninists. Thus Manuilsky, the Ukrainian Communist leader who at that time was prominent in the Comintern bureaucracy, complained at the Tenth Comintern Plenum in 1929:

> How does it happen that all the fundamental problems of the Communist International fail to stir our fraternal British party? It is not that the British Communist Party does not pass resolutions or take a stand upon all important questions. No, this cannot be said. Nevertheless, one does not feel any profound organic connection with all the problems of the world Labour movement. All these problems have the appearance of being forcibly injected into the activities of the British Communist Party. In late years we have seen everywhere intensive political discussions. How many questions were passionately discussed, let us say, in the Communist Party of Germany? The German comrades carefully weigh every word

[1] For a realistic account of the relations of the C.I. and the Russian party see R. Sorge in C. A. Willoughby, *Sorge: Soviet Master Spy* (1952), pp. 127-33.

spoken by anybody. They allow no deviation from the line, they attack the least deviation, respecting no persons. A series of such great discussions we have also seen in the Communist Party of Poland. Yet in the British party there is a sort of special system which may be characterised thus: the party is a society of great friends.[1]

What Manuilsky said was true enough: instead of splitting up along the lines of 'left' and 'right' tendencies, the members of the C.P.G.B. Executive not infrequently judged matters on their merits, and there was much cross-voting on questions of policy. While the leadership of the Russian and other parties was being decimated by expulsions, the British functionaries mostly remained loyal to each other, and the old Clydeside group, especially MacManus, Campbell, and Bell, formed a hard core of influential officials, controlling the party with the assistance of the rather colourless Albert Inkpin, who was still acting as secretary, and of a few newcomers such as Andrew Rothstein and Arthur Horner.

So long as the British party made progress and increased its membership as it did between 1924 and 1927, this solidarity of control did not provide much excuse for Comintern intervention, and, as we have seen, in this period the C.P.G.B. was repeatedly praised for its 'correct tactics'. But the decline of the party's membership in 1927 and 1928 made the Moscow Secretariat feel that something was wrong in Britain, and the natural scapegoat was the C.P.G.B. leadership. The Comintern itself was now changing its tactics, partly as a result of the fight of factions inside the Russian party and partly as a result of the situation in China, where the 'united front' policy had been of more value to the Nationalists under Chiang Kai Shek than to the Chinese Communists. Towards the end of 1927 a new policy was evolved in Moscow – a policy entitled, with unconscious irony, 'Class Against Class'. This meant in practice a move in the direction of sectarianism: the Communist parties were expected to attack the Social-Democrats as 'Social Fascists', and to regard them as enemies no better than – and in some cases worse than – the mem-

[1] *Inprecorr*, ix, 1140.

bers of the capitalist parties. The British party as usual found itself in difficulties over the change of policy, and its lack of adaptability was naturally taken as a serious fault in Moscow. In fact, the curiously rigid state of the British party was largely the result of the earlier attempt to 'Bolshevise' the party, which meant, to apply the Russian model in Britain without sufficient regard for local circumstances.

For there was no doubt about it that the British party was not really capable of becoming a 'Bolshevik' party. It is true that its organisation at the top conformed to the Comintern pattern, which was based on the model of the Russian party. There was a 'Politburo' and an 'Orgburo', both with numerous 'departments' all constantly receiving instructions from Moscow and passing them on to the District Committees; there was a Control Commission of three or four, whose job it was to audit the party accounts and to hear appeals[1]; there was a Comintern representative, as already stated, with his own staff. But all this organisation at the top was too much for a party with a membership of only a few thousands. The instructions were passed down, but they were not effectively obeyed, for the leaders of the party were divorced from the rank and file, busy travelling to and from Moscow, or sitting in the London office in King Street compiling information to send to the Comintern and deciphering instructions received. Consequently, at the local level, not enough was done. The party channels of communication became choked with unfulfilled orders: the party was as Arthur Horner put it 'constipated'.[2] It was no wonder that new recruits swiftly fell away, disappointed by the absence of effective internal democracy.

*   *   *

The new tactics of the Comintern had developed in 1927, but owing to a 'technical mishap'[3] – possibly the arrest of a messenger – they were not received in Britain in time to influence the 1927

---

[1] See, e.g., CP, *Report of the Control Commission*, 1924.
[2] *Inprecorr*, ix, 1075.
[3] The phrase is R. Page Arnot's, from his article 'Ten Years of the C.P.G.B.', *DW*, 11 Aug. 1930.

Congress of the C.P.G.B. It was not until the Ninth Plenum of the Comintern in Moscow in February 1928 that the British leaders discovered what had happened. In accordance with precedent special Commissions were held during this conference to discuss the problems and future policy of each individual party. Each Commission was composed of all the delegates at the conference from the party concerned, but it was normal for the representatives of the party concerned to be outnumbered by officials of the Comintern headquarters and specially appointed members from the delegations of other countries. We are told that at this particular Commission on the British party the sessions 'were marked by passion and tenseness'[1] and this is borne out by the record of the debates[2]; but as usual a unanimous report emerged. It was accepted that the party should 'adopt clearer and sharper tactics of opposition' to the Labour Party and the trade union leadership.[3] In accordance with the principle of democratic centralism, the British leaders had no option but to accept this decision, once it had been voted on by the whole conference, and to apply it as best they could when they got home.

Nevertheless, it was obvious to the Comintern officials that the C.P.G.B. delegates, though paying lip-service to the new Moscow 'line', were full of misgivings and mental reservations. This became even clearer at the Sixth World Congress of the Comintern, which was held in July of the same year. The World Congress was an important occasion for the British party, for it involved a thorough discussion of the colonial question. The Comintern Secretariat presented a colonial thesis which argued that imperialist powers prevented the industrialisation of their colonies. But the British Communists knew well enough that this was by no means entirely true: their only Member of Parliament, Shapurji Saklatvala, was a scion of the Tata family, which had built up a large steel industry in India. They accordingly produced major criticisms of the official resolution proposed by Kuusinen. After a warm debate, in the course of which the British speakers were accused of chauvinism, their amendments were put to the

---

[1] *Inprecorr*, viii, 249.
[2] ECCI, *Communist Policy in Great Britain* (1928).   [3] ECCI, *op. cit.*, p. 192.

vote and heavily defeated; and they departed from Moscow in high dudgeon after issuing a curious statement criticising the way that the debate had been conducted:

We wish to enter our emphatic protest against the tone and method of polemics introduced by Comrade Kuusinen and certain other comrades, which, if persisted in, can only have the effect of killing healthy discussions. The only possible method of discussion for the Communist International, in our opinion, is to debate questions upon their merits, with full freedom and encouragement for all sections and individual comrades to state their point of view freely, frankly, and fraternally. The method of hurrying to tie labels on comrades who hold different opinions, before a final decision has been reached, can only result in destroying independent thought and in robbing the Comintern discussions of much of their value.[1]

This rearguard plea for freedom of discussion – an unexpected revelation of original grace – can have made little impression on the Comintern officials, who were already fashioning an alternative leadership for the British party. They wished in particular to reduce the influence of Campbell, who since appearing as a national figure in 1924 had become the party's most prominent member, especially after the death of MacManus in 1927.[2] They thought that Dutt and Pollitt would prove a suitable and more pliant team. Dutt was felt to have a firm grasp of theoretical questions and could discourse at almost endless length on the various 'tendencies' inside the Comintern. Pollitt had complementary qualities: although a poor theoretician, he was a good organiser and a powerful popular orator: as secretary of the Minority Movement he was already in a key post in the party. The Comintern officials' confidence in Pollitt was shown early in 1929 by his despatch to New York as one of their two emissaries to effect a change in the control of the American Communist Party.[3]

But Dutt and Pollitt, by themselves, could not overthrow the

[1] *Inprecorr*, viii, 1744.
[2] MacManus's ashes were placed in the wall of the Red Square, Moscow. Bell, *Pioneering Days*, p. 229.
[3] Pollitt in *DW*, 27 Mar. 1934; B. Gitlow, *I Confess* (New York, 1940), pp. 515-19.

existing British leadership, especially as Dutt was chronically ill and had been living on the continent for several years. To swing the balance, the Comintern leaders made use of the British Young Communist League, which was under the close supervision of its Swedish counterpart, acting as the agent of the Young Communist International.[1] The leading spirits of the Y.C.L. were for the most part ambitious young men of working-class origin who had never had any other political allegiance than that of international Communism. Among them were William Rust, Walter Tapsell and David Springhall – Londoners all, who owed their entire careers to the party and who were very different types from the Scottish artisans who had come into the party with the B.S.P. and S.L.P. This new group was in action against the executive at the British Party Congress in January 1929; but as yet there was little cohesion in their ranks, and at an open election the existing leadership could still secure re-election after having given undertakings to accept the new Comintern 'line'. The Comintern officials, however, were far from satisfied with this outcome, and at once despatched a private letter to the C.P.G.B. saying that:

> The new E.C. chosen as a result of free election is to us a matter of consternation. . . . The situation manifested at the Congress demanded, above all, that new elements be brought into the ranks of the Executive. The Congress has shown that it is precisely in the British party that the danger arises that a small group of leaders may develop which will be insufficiently linked up with active party life and the active struggles of the workers.[2]

This was an unkind cut, for if the British leaders were isolated from 'active party life' it was because they had been kept too busy by Moscow. Their response to this missive was to remove from the Politburo two members who were neither firm Comintern men nor firm adherents of the old gang – namely, Gallacher and Murphy. This provoked an immediate intervention from the Y.C.L., which had assumed the role of Comintern watchdog. In a letter to the Politburo the Y.C.L. demanded an immediate request by the British party to the Comintern to establish a Com-

[1] B. Hallström, *I Believed in Moscow* (1935), pp. 29f.   [2] *Inprecorr*, ix, 885.

mission 'to consider the whole question of the leadership of the
C.P.G.B.'; and then an early party conference to 'consider the
findings of the C.I. Commission and elect a new party leadership
for the carrying through of the new line and the Comintern
letter'.[1]

The dispute, which had now created serious divisions inside the
British party, was still unresolved when the Tenth Plenum of the
Comintern took place in Moscow in July. The British leaders
attended in order to defend themselves, and Rust was allowed to
be present under the auspices of the Y.C.L. Rust assumed the role
of informer and prosecutor of the C.P.G.B. and denounced the
leadership of his own party with a boldness hardly explicable
except on the assumption that he was already sure of the support
of the Comintern officials. Campbell defended himself as best he
could, pointing out that the British party had been 'swimming
against the stream' in its campaigns for membership and influence.[2] Bell, Horner, and even to a certain extent Pollitt, spoke
on his behalf. But Manuilsky for the Comintern Secretariat
brought down the scales on Rust's side. Dutt and Page Arnot, he
said, were the only correct theoreticians in the British party. The
existing committee had made serious errors, had been too sympathetic to non-Communist 'left-wingers' such as Maxton and
Cook, had failed to build up factory nuclei, and so on.[3] This intervention was decisive: Campbell and his colleagues were forced
to agree to an immediate and unconstitutional reorganisation of
the Politburo, and to the summoning of a special Party Congress.
The Comintern Executive addressed a special letter to this Congress, which met in November 1929: 'The opportunist elements
in the party leadership', it stated, 'hindered the reorganisation of
the party on a factory basis. . . . These elements must be brought
out into the open and ruthlessly exposed.'[4] The letter was signed by
Thälmann (Germany), Garlandi (Italy), and Sémard (France), but
not by any of the Russians, lest it appear too openly that the
Russian party was dictating to the Comintern. Meanwhile, meetings of district memberships of the British party had been held to

---

[1] *Ibid.*, ix, 1363f.   [2] *Ibid.*, ix, 873.   [3] *Ibid.*, ix, 1139f.
[4] CP, *Resolutions of the Eleventh Congress* (1929), p. 40.

demand changes in accordance with the Comintern directives, and thus to give a semblance of popular initiative to what was in reality a *coup d'état* from above.[1]

When the special Party Congress met in November there was a foregone conclusion to the discussions. Just in case there still remained a possibility of the membership re-electing the old leaders, the system of voting for the Central Committee was changed. According to an account by Page Arnot:

> For the first time in the history of the party, instead of the so-called 'democratic' open vote of Congress (really Social Democratic method, because its only effect was to ensure the yearly re-election without an ounce of political discussion, of those whose names had been most prominently before the party) a Bolshevik method was adopted. For the purpose of drawing up the C.C. list a nominations commission was elected by the Congress. The political qualifications of each candidate were discussed exhaustively. . . . A list containing twelve of the old Central Committee and 23 new members was adopted by the Congress, with one addition. Amongst those who were not re-elected were Comrades Inkpin, Rothstein, Horner, Bell.[2]

Campbell remained on the Central Committee but was not elected to the Politburo; and Pollitt became general secretary in place of Inkpin. There were no resignations or expulsions, for the time being: to that extent the party was still 'a society of friends'. But the real essence of democratic control had gone. Pollitt, under the guidance of Dutt, was the Comintern's man in charge: in a few years' time he would be officially described as the 'leader' of the party. Almost at once the publication of the *Daily Worker* began: the Comintern had imposed upon the new leadership the initial task of founding a daily paper not later than the First of January 1930.[3] Its editor – appointed for political reasons, for he had no journalistic experience – was William Rust; and the business manager was Walter Tapsell, also of the Y.C.L. Thus, as in the French party, a new Stalinist leadership had come to power,

[1] *Workers' Life*, 26 July 1929; *Communist Review*, i, 568–78.
[2] *Inprecorr*, x, 47.
[3] Resolution of ECCI Polit-Secretariat, *Inprecorr*, ix, 1126.

and the instrument of the *coup d'état* had been the younger generation.[1] Through many vicissitudes of policy and circumstance, it
was to remain in control practically unchanged until well after
the great Russian dictator had passed away.

[1] G. Walter, *Histoire du Parti Communiste Français* (Paris, 1948), pp. 227f.

CHAPTER IV

'CLASS AGAINST CLASS', 1929-33

WITH the British party reduced to an almost slavish submission
to Moscow, the control of the Comintern over its policies could
assume a quasi-military character. At Moscow the Anglo-
American Secretariat and its parallel organisation, the Anglo-
American Section of the Profintern, transmitted detailed instructions for the British leaders on the conduct of their operations.
These bodies drew their information from a variety of sources.
There were, first of all, the agents of the Comintern or of the
Profintern who visited Britain on permanent or temporary
mission. As we have seen, Petrovsky was the permanent Comintern representative in Britain between 1924 and 1929, and seems
to have been very successful in evading the police; but other
agents had some difficulty in entering the country without being
caught, and Scotland Yard acquired a high reputation in Comintern circles for its skill in this respect.[1] Nevertheless, many representatives either of the Comintern or of the Profintern did
enter Britain for long enough periods to enable them to collect
information of value to the officials in Moscow.

Apart from this direct reconnaisance by its own agents, the
Comintern naturally drew the bulk of its detailed information
from members of the British party. There were, in the first place,
the British representatives permanently or semi-permanently
attached to the Comintern and Profintern staffs, who could be
used for drafting instructions, interpreting local conditions, and
translating. Then there were the leaders of the British party who
were so constantly visiting the Russian capital for conferences of
one sort or another: the extent of this coming and going may be
gauged from Pollitt's claim in 1930 to have visited the U.S.S.R.

[1] J. Valtin, *Out of the Night* (New York, 1941), p. 341; Willoughby, *Sorge:
Soviet Master Spy*, p. 60.

54

no less than twenty-seven times since 1921.[1] Then there were the
regular confidential reports of the C.P.G.B., the Minority Movement, and other British organisations on their own activities:
these reports were drawn up on Moscow specifications and were
often extremely detailed; but by the time they reached Moscow
they might well be a little out-of-date. Finally, there were the
publications of the British Communist press, which were closely
scrutinised in Moscow both for news of the British movement
and for evidence of the quality of British Communist propaganda
and its adherence to the current 'line'.

It was natural that in this new 'period' – according to the Communist theorists, the 'third period' since the revolution – there
should be a concentration of party activities and of Moscow
directives on the industrial side of the movement. In the purely
political sphere, many of the avenues of approach to 'the masses'
had in fact been severed by the 'new line' of 'Class Against Class'.
The Labour Party Conference had already reacted by forbidding
Communists to attend its sessions in future even as trade-union
delegates[2]; and, as we have seen, the Communists themselves had
'liquidated' the National Left Wing, leaving a certain number of
non-Communist sympathisers with no option save that of joining
the Communist Party themselves (which very few of them did)
or of returning to a fuller loyalty to the Labour Party. Even the
British section of the League Against Imperialism, which had had
James Maxton of the I.L.P. as its chairman, and which was
supposed to be a broad organisation of all those opposed to imperialism, had conformed to the 'new line' to the extent of ex-
pelling Maxton – a move which, by making its Communist control transparent to all save the most gullible of its members, led
to a considerable loss of influence.[3] The organ of the I.L.P., the
New Leader, commenting on Maxton's expulsion, said that it was

. . . final proof of the impossibility of working with Communists
while they remain in their present state of mind, except upon terms
of absolute subservience to their narrow and stupid ukases.[4]

[1] *DW*, 28 Aug. 1930.   [2] Labour Party *Report*, 1928, pp. 162-7.
[3] *The Times*, 20 Sept. 1929.   [4] *New Leader*, 27 Sept. 1929.

It was no wonder that Pollitt had to admit in 1930 that the 'transmission belts' were 'turning no wheels' and that as for the 'bridges to the masses', there were 'only the same faithful few going over them in every case'.[1]

The Minority Movement was one of the 'transmission belts' seriously weakened by the estrangement of the Communists from the Labour Left, but at first its remaining members still had their links with the rank-and-file of the unions, and they now had the task of building up an 'independent leadership of the working class', which should provide an alternative to the existing trade-union bureaucracy. The immediate effect of this policy, when first applied in 1928, was the establishment of two 'break-away' unions under Communist control. One of them was the United Mineworkers of Scotland, which was founded by the Fife miners, who as we have seen had for some years been discontented with the existing union structure. The other was the United Clothing Workers, a body of East End Jews who had long been dissatisfied with the policy of the United Garment Workers Union, partly because it had its headquarters not in London but in Leeds and was largely run by Irishmen. Here at least was something to show for the 'new line', although to set against it was the loss of sympathisers in other trades, for union-splitting tactics were inevitably highly unpopular in a country with a strong tradition of homogeneous unionism.

Unfortunately for the party, neither of the two new unions ever made very much headway. The United Mineworkers of Scotland, in spite of its title, won few recruits outside Fife, where it was based, and was quite unable to secure the elimination of the older Scottish miners' organisation.[2] The United Clothing Workers suffered from serious inner dissensions, resulting in the expulsion of its founder, Sam Elsbury, a Russian-born Jew of considerable ability as a speaker and organiser. Elsbury objected to the use of the Union for directly political purposes, and soon found himself

---

[1] *DW*, 1 Sept. 1930.
[2] R. P. Arnot, *The Scottish Miners* (1955), p. 213. Arnot omits the role of the RILU and of the CP, for which see Campbell's report at the Tenth Plenum in Moscow, *Inprecorr*, ix, 1228f.

TENTH NATIONAL CONGRESS, BERMONDSEY, JANUARY 1929

denounced as a 'social fascist' and expelled both from the party and from his post as union secretary.[1]

The trouble was that the Minority Movement, though by no means a negligible force at the outset, was nevertheless a very small nucleus for a campaign designed to form an alternative leadership for the entire working class. Early in 1931, for instance, it was reported that the Communist membership of the Minority Movement, constituting almost the whole body of its active workers, was only seven hundred.[2] Yet there was a ponderous superstructure at Moscow to watch the progress of its work and to determine the character of its future tasks. Margaret McCarthy, who served in the Anglo-American Section of the Profintern, has described how the work of this body was conducted.[3]

The Moscow Secretariat of the organisation was now being supervised by a 'troika' consisting of Lozovsky, a Ukrainian Jew, Kastanyan, a Georgian, and Fritz Emmerich, a German. Emmerich was in charge of the Anglo-American Section, but in practice he was very much in the hands of his principal secretary, a Polish Jewess named Barishnik, described by Margaret McCarthy as 'beautiful, languorous, green-eyed', but also apparently very able. It was Barishnik who drew up directives for the various Communist-controlled industrial organisations in Britain – the United Clothing Workers, the United Mineworkers of Scotland, the National Unemployed Workers Movement and the various sections of the Minority Movement. Of course, she and her fellow-functionaries had to follow the 'line' as it was laid down by Stalin and his closest advisers; and the Profintern directives reveal the usual bureaucratic tendency to 'hedge' by touching on all types of possible activity which the parties could pursue, so that any future change in Communist tactics could be discovered to be implicit in the existing instructions to the parties. A good example of this occurred in an Open Letter from the Red International to the Minority Movement in April 1931, which

---

[1] *Worker's Life*, 20 Dec. 1929; S. Lerner, 'History of the United Clothing Workers Union', unpublished Ph.D. thesis, London University, 1956, pp. 379ff.
[2] *Inprecorr*, xi, 672.
[3] M. McCarthy, *Generation in Revolt* (1953), pp. 165-71.

E

mentioned the importance of work inside the existing trade union organisations, but without any special emphasis, as this was still the period of agitation for 'independent leadership'.[1] When at the end of the same year the 'line' changed, and importance was again attached to the need for work among the 'rank-and-file trade union supporters', it was possible for the leaders in Moscow to claim that in their resolution this point had already been 'very strongly emphasised' as early as April, although in fact it had only been a single paragraph in a text of several thousand words.[2] There were other instances of this type of covering tactics on the part of the Moscow functionaries.

*   *   *

To their credit, not all the British Communists settled down very happily to these conditions of detailed supervision, in spite of the *bouleversement* of the leadership in 1929. The least happy, naturally, were those who had been accused of 'trade-union legalism' – that is, paying more attention to the interests of the unions than to those of the party – and who were now obliged to adapt themselves to the idea of 'independent leadership' of the working class.

In South Wales, 'trade union legalism' had been especially strong, for as Arthur Horner realised, the union lodges were in many ways an important element of the life of the mining villages. It seems that at first, after his exclusion from the Central Committee at the end of 1929, he and his friends stood aside from the activity of the party, for the South Wales District Committee early in 1930 plunged into an excess of zeal for the 'new line' which far exceeded the bounds of practicability. In April it sent out a circular calling for 'mass political strikes' in order to assist a strike of woollen workers in Yorkshire, an issue not likely to carry much weight with the bulk of the Welsh miners. The Politburo was obliged to step in to countermand this order, declaring:

> This dangerous 'left' sectarianism arises directly from the widespread 'right' opportunism, which is the chief danger.[3]

[1] *Worker*, 2 May 1931.   [2] *Ibid.*, 16 Apr. 1932.
[3] *DW*, 12 June 1930.

This was a not untypical example of the language and method of reasoning now in vogue among the leaders. To set things right, it seemed necessary to change the composition of the South Wales District Committee, and this could of course easily be done by the method of 'Bolshevik Democracy' which had transformed the Politburo itself in 1929. A South Wales District Congress was accordingly held which, we are told, was 'different from all previous Congresses' in that 'it had been prepared beforehand'. The 'preparation' consisted in having an agreed list of candidates chosen by a 'Panels Commission'. As the *Daily Worker* report put it, 'This was the first time that the District Party Committee was elected by such procedure, and the results certainly justified the method. . . . Seven members of the old D.P.C. have been removed.'[1] Among those who now assumed the major responsibilities in the area were Charles Stead and Leonard Jefferies, who had lately returned from courses of instruction at the Lenin School at Moscow.

This did not end the difficulties of the Communists in South Wales, for Horner was still their principal leader among the miners, and he had to be persuaded to set a good example by accepting the application of the 'new line' in the coalfield, where at the end of 1930 official strike action was imminent. The Fifth Congress of the Profintern in August had laid it down that 'independent leadership of the working class' involved the formation by the Communists and their sympathisers of 'struggle committees' to prepare for strike action, and 'strike committees' to run the strike; and it was stated that these committees were to be independent of the existing trade-union leadership.[2] This policy might have worked even in South Wales if there had been enough Communists to go round; but at this time their numbers were far too few to implement such a policy. But the new District Committee was obliged to make the attempt, and first of all, in order to remove the 'pessimism and passivity' of many of the South Wales Communists, Horner was prevailed upon to make a public confession of his own 'errors':

[1] *DW*, 18 June 1930.
[2] RILU, *Resolutions of the Fifth World Congress* (1931), p. 86.

The new leadership of the Communist Party (he declared) acted quite correctly in the course taken against the foremost members of the old leadership. Only by such steps as were taken was it possible to get the party swung into the fight for independent leadership of the working class.[1]

In an actual situation involving strike action, however, Horner found it impossible to carry out the line of 'independent leadership'. The South Wales Miners Federation was faced by an employers' lock-out in January 1931, and after a Minority Movement conference in Cardiff a Central Strike Committee was set up in the approved fashion, with Horner as its chairman. But he had no stomach for the fight, realising how weak the forces at his disposal were. He opposed the election of an independent strike committee at Glynneath, resigned the chairmanship of the Central Strike Committee, and refused to attend a meeting of the Profintern Secretariat to defend himself. He explained that the local strike committees that he had set up alongside the regular union apparatus were 'without mass content, resulting only in our isolation'. As for help from London, Horner declared, 'If no headquarters existed we would have experienced only a slightly greater absence of assistance.'[2]

When the strike had collapsed, as it soon did, the Politburo took Horner to task on a number of counts. The indictment was published in the *Daily Worker*:

> His opposition to the line, his lack of faith in the masses, his failure to understand the depth of the capitalist crisis and the prospects of revolutionary struggle, his cowardly retreat before the bureaucracy, his anarchistic flouting of Communist discipline, stamp him as the most outspoken champion of opportunism within the party.[3]

Horner wavered in the face of the attack, which was reinforced by hasty resolutions of condemnation from other districts of the party. In March he accepted the view that the 'path of revolutionary duty' lay in 'submission to the party'[4]; but the form in which

---

[1] *DW*, 25 Sept. 1930.
[2] Remarks at South Wales District Committee meeting, 17 Jan. 1931, reported *DW*, 10 Mar. 1931.
[3] *DW*, 11 Mar. 1931.   [4] Letter of 19 Mar. quoted *DW*, 27 Apr. 1931.

he was expected to make his submission distressed him, and a few weeks later he was again in revolt at the 'deceit' involved and the danger of 'perpetuating these weaknesses',[1] although by this time the long-range guns of Lozovsky himself had been brought into play to denounce him personally for his 'open opportunist position'.[2] In June he appeared before the Central Committee of the party and spoke for two hours, explaining why he refused to accept the standpoint of the Politburo; but of course the Central Committee had no real independence, and the matter was referred back to the Politburo with permission to take up with the Comintern the question of Horner's expulsion from the party.[3] Horner's popularity in South Wales made the leadership very unwilling to proceed to such an extreme measure; and in the end he was induced to make a statement accepting the Comintern and Central Committee resolutions 'as being a correct analysis of my mistakes'.[4] But this was not until November 1931, so that it had taken two full years finally to reconcile the most important of the South Wales Communists to the full implications of 'Class Against Class'.

*   *   *

In the industrial North of England the situation was in some respects similar, although 'trade-union legalism' was limited by the almost complete absence of Communist footholds in the principal unions. In Lancashire the party had never secured more than a very few adherents outside of Liverpool and Manchester; and the Manchester membership tended to be dominated by a young Jewish group which had few contacts with the workers in the cotton and mining industries.[5] It was with a view to correcting this situation that in 1929 Frank Bright, a miner, was brought in from South Wales to act as Lancashire organiser.[6] Unfortunately, Bright sided with the Central Committee majority and so was

[1] Letter of 15 Apr., quoted *ibid.*
[2] Open letter to members of the Minority Movement, quoted *DW*, 12 Apr. 1931.
[3] *DW*, 9 June 1931.   [4] *DW*, 6 Nov. 1931.
[5] McCarthy, *op. cit.*, pp. 71-4.   [6] *Workers' Life*, 8 Feb. 1929.

discredited for the 'new period'; and at the beginning of 1930 there was a complete absence of effective leadership in the area. Early in the year the Manchester District Committee seriously proposed that there should be a march of workers to Burnley Barracks to 'call on the soldiers in uniform to demonstrate with the workers in the streets'. The inadvisability of this proposal arose from two facts: there were not a dozen members of the party in Burnley, and there were no longer any soldiers stationed in the town.[1]

During the two succeeding years there were plenty of opportunities for recruiting members of the party in Lancashire and Yorkshire, but the existing membership was incapable of exploiting them. Unemployment was widespread and the textile industry was in acute distress: desperate strikes of spinners and weavers took place against the almost inevitable wage cuts and other economies made by the employers. But the Communists were neither numerous enough nor able enough to take advantage of the situation: or if they did secure some small advantage, they came up against the inveterate conservatism of the working class, and the stout Nonconformist or Catholic religious enthusiasms, which prevented them from retaining any temporary influence. Thus in the spring of 1930 the Minority Movement was able to play a prominent part in a woollen strike in the Bradford area: Ernie Brown, the party organiser, was chairman of the Bradford Central Strike Committee, and the Workers International Relief, which was one of the 'satellite' organisations, attracted some notice by its work for the strikers.[2] Yet it proved impossible to get any 'mill committees' organised, independently of the unions, as the approved Profintern procedure required. As John Mahon, the party industrial organiser, later admitted, the strikers felt that both the Minority Movement and the Communist Party were impositions from outside – as indeed they were. Mahon confessed that it was a tactical error to brandish the slogan of the 'struggle for power' to strikers who were only anxious for a small improvement in their economic conditions. The result of the strike, he admitted, was that:

[1] *Communist Review*, ii, 244.   [2] *Worker*, 23 May 1930.

The workers went back with their ranks broken and not under our leadership, and we have since failed to register any organisational development.[1]

This sort of cycle of events was repeated again and again in the textile areas. The party proved itself incapable of recruiting the victims of the most genuine economic distress. A further example is provided by the struggle against the introduction of the eight-loom system among the Lancashire weavers – an attempt at 'rationalisation' and increased productivity at a time when almost half the labour force was unemployed. Endeavouring to profit from the mistakes of the Yorkshire strike, the Lancashire Communists set up 'Councils of Action' at Burnley, Blackburn and Todmorden to prepare the strike beforehand. These bodies were in fact the 'struggle committees' which the Profintern prescribed as a prerequisite of strike action. A strike took place early in 1931, and was successful to a considerable degree in securing the postponement of the introduction of the eight-loom system.[2] Yet even in these circumstances the party hardly made any progress. Its members had made several mistakes which had not passed unnoticed, one of which was to link the fight against the eight-loom system with such impractical demands as that for an overall minimum wage of £2.[3] Ernie Woolley, the Lancashire party leader, lamented the hesitancy and confusion of the Minority Movement group, which attempted vainly to win effective control of the situation from the established trade unions.[4]

*   *   * .

It might have been supposed that the Communists would do best among the unemployed, whose numbers rose to such formidable proportions in these years. In this sphere, after all, there were no established unions to face, and the best-known organisation claiming to represent the interests of the unemployed was the National Unemployed Workers' Movement, the former

[1] *Ibid.*, 3 Jan. 1931.   [2] See *Worker*, Jan. and Feb. 1931.
[3] *Ibid.*, 12 Dec. 1931. Many of the weavers were earning more than £2.
[4] *Ibid.*, 13 June 1931; cf. John Mahon in *RILU Magazine*, 15 June 1932, p. 517f.

N.U.W.C.M. which had always been under effective Communist control. For a time in the middle-twenties this body had actually been recognised by the T.U.C., at least to the extent of establishing a joint committee for liaison purposes. This arrangement, however, was broken off by the T.U.C. General Council, which in 1928 declared itself dissatisfied with 'the bona-fides of the organisation'.[1] Still, the N.U.W.M. was the one body which agitated fiercely on behalf of the unemployed as such, and the Labour Party and T.U.C. were inhibited from setting up any organisation of their own because the individual trade unions claimed each to represent their own unemployed members. There were, indeed, plenty of grievances for the unemployed to concern themselves with, and not least their treatment at the hands of the Labour Party leadership: the Blanesburgh Report of 1927, which was signed by Margaret Bondfield and Frank Hodges among others, proposed a considerable reduction in unemployment benefits in order to reduce the debt incurred by the Unemployment Insurance Fund. Further economies at the expense of the unemployed followed under the Labour Government of 1929-31, culminating in the drastic cuts recommended by the May Committee which even the T.U.C. refused to accept.

From the party point of view, the trouble with the N.U.W.M. was that its leaders, even though they were Communists, tended to look upon the problems of their membership as their first task, and so became absorbed in the technicalities of unemployment relief from the point of view of individual grievances, instead of striving constantly to build up a mass movement for political ends. This sort of behaviour, which was similar to the 'trade-union legalism' which had already aroused the wrath of the Comintern, was itself vigorously condemned at the Fifth Congress of the Profintern in Moscow in 1930. The Congress denounced these 'opportunistic tendencies' which had the effect of 'opposing the development of the N.U.W.M. into a mass organisation', and demanded a more active recruiting campaign.[2] Wal Hannington and his colleagues did their best to respond to this pressure, and in

[1] T.U.C. *Report*, 1928, p. 113.
[2] RILU, *Resolutions of the Fifth World Congress*, p. 112.

1931 launched a strenuous campaign of mass demonstrations, hunger marches and the like. The campaign was greatly assisted by the crisis of the Labour Government in August, and largely because of this the N.U.W.M. membership expanded from 20,000 in the summer to 37,000 at the end of the year – still, of course, only a tiny proportion of an unemployed army which now numbered about three millions.[1] The pressure from Russia continued, and in April 1932 the chairman of the organisation, Sid Elias, was summoned to Moscow, where he stayed for six months as an 'adviser' in the Anglo-American Section of the Profintern. Elias seems virtually to have been a hostage in Moscow: he did not know how long he was to be kept there, and it was simply his task to demand reports from his colleagues in London and to send them instructions for bigger and more lavish demonstrations, involving larger numbers of workers. In one letter to London he emphasised the need for expanding the size of the hunger marches, which up till then, as he said, had 'involved at the most one or two thousand out of millions of unemployed'.[2] It was evidently the intention of his superiors in Moscow to turn the unemployed movement in Britain into a directly revolutionary organisation. But in spite of some unpleasant local disorders, notably that at Birkenhead in September 1932, and those in London in October-November arising out of the biggest of the hunger marches, these hopes remained unfulfilled.

*   *   *

At the end of 1931 it was becoming apparent even in Moscow that the 'Class Against Class' policy meant, not the consolidation of Communist control over the European working class, but rather the alienation of the parties from any general influence whatsoever. In Germany the principal benefactor of the hostility of Social-Democrats and Communists was the National-Socialist Party; and in France the Communist Party had shrunk to a tiny

[1] Hannington's report to Eighth Session of Profintern Central Council, *RILU Magazine*, 1 Feb. 1932, p. 64.
[2] Letter from Elias to N.U.W.M., quoted by counsel at Elias's trial for incitement, *Morning Post*, 9 Nov. 1932.

fraction of its membership in the early nineteen-twenties. So far as Britain was concerned, the party's influence in the trade-union movement, which had received so much praise in Moscow at the time of the General Strike, had now almost disappeared, and the Minority Movement hardly extended beyond the exiguous Communist membership. Willie Allan, who went to Moscow to represent the Movement, was obliged to admit that

> Throughout the whole of 1930 there was a steady falling-away in membership of the National Minority Movement, and a much deeper fall in its influence and standing among the trade unionists and in the trade-union organisation.[1]

Part of the trouble was that the members of the party, few as they were, were overburdened by innumerable 'tasks' imposed upon them by the Comintern. The heaviest of these was probably that of maintaining the *Daily Worker* circulation, which must have posed an exceptional problem in view of the refusal of the established newspaper distributors to handle it. Each industrial member of the party also had his responsibilities in connection with the remaining 'satellite' organisations, such as the Unemployed Movement, the International Class War Prisoners Aid, and the Friends of the Soviet Union. The last-named was part of an international admiration society which had been set up under Communist control in Moscow in 1927.[2] Regular work in many of these bodies, as well as activity in the local Communist 'cell' and a certain amount of 'fraction' work, naturally exhausted even the most devoted members of the party; and it was not surprising that special *ad hoc* campaigns, such as that for the 'Workers' Charter' in 1931, which was designed to appeal widely among the industrial workers, collapsed very quickly after reaching the climax of a national demonstration. The Charter Campaign led to the formation of numerous 'Charter Committees' throughout the country, and culminated in a 'National Convention' in London, but within two or three months all the committees had disappeared and the party was as isolated as before.[3]

[1] *Communist Review*, iv, 473.
[2] For its early history see A. Inkpin, *Friends of the U.S.S.R.* (1942).
[3] *Communist Review*, iv, 474.

It is true that the British Communists were able to claim impressive increases of membership in the months following the fall of the Labour Government in August 1931. The defection of Ramsay MacDonald and several of his leading colleagues to form a coalition government with the Conservatives and Liberals shook the faith of many Labour Party supporters, and the role of the New York bankers in the immediate crisis seemed to confirm the Marxist view that, in the last resort, international capitalism could find ways and means of thwarting democratic policies. A few weeks later the so-called 'Invergordon Mutiny' directed attention to the party, for although the seamen's demonstrations were not initiated by Communists and were entirely the product of harsh and inequitable cuts in their pay, it suited the government to claim that Communist propaganda had been a major cause, and it suited the Communists to claim the credit thus offered to them. The principal leaders of the disturbances were discharged from the Navy shortly afterwards, and two or three of them, who had been made much of at Communist demonstrations, later joined the party.[1]

It is not surprising, therefore, that by the time of the General Election in November 1931 the party membership had doubled. But the total was still insignificant, especially in view of the character of the crisis. With the Labour Party split by the desertion of its leaders, and with an unemployment total climbing towards three millions, a Communist Party of only 6,000 seemed almost ludicrous.[2] The new recruits added little to the party, for being mostly unemployed, they could not pay their dues; and it seemed only too evident that when the immediate crisis was over they would drift away from the party, as the miners had done after the 1926 strike.

Certainly it needed an almost incredible combination of blindness and optimism to obtain any comfort from the General Election results. The Labour Party, of course, suffered enormous losses to the 'National' Government candidates, but its constituency organisation remained virtually intact, and it still had a

---

[1] One of them was Fred Copeman. See his *Reason in Revolt* (1948), p. 53.
[2] *Inprecorr*, xii, 447.

popular vote of six and a half millions. By contrast, the Communists could secure only 75,000 votes for their twenty-six candidates and were unable to win a single seat. Only in eight constituencies did they secure more than one-fifth of the poll of the Labour candidates. Yet, according to Dutt, writing immediately afterwards in the *Daily Worker*,

> The workers have lost confidence in the Labour Party, and seek elsewhere. . . . The Labour movement, the old Labour movement, is dying. The workers' movement, the independent workers' movement, is rising.[1]

This absurd conclusion aroused the wrath of J. T. Murphy, who was now the only potential rival of the Dutt-Pollitt leadership inside the party. He poured scorn upon Dutt's optimism, enquiring what could be said for the C.P.G.B., with its 75,000 votes, if the Labour Party with six and a half million was dying.[2] After this it was not long before he was eased out of his position in the central leadership in the party and faced with the alternatives of expulsion or reduction to a subordinate post. In March 1932 he ventured to propose the idea of British credits to the Soviet Union so as to absorb the unemployed of his home town, Sheffield, on industrial orders for Russia.[3] This proposal, sensible as it was, outran the existing party brief and was seized upon by his colleagues in the Politburo as an opportunity to make an example of this too independent 'comrade'. Murphy was ordered to sign a public recantation: he refused, and promptly resigned from the party.[4] He was at once denounced as a 'deserter from the ranks of Communism', and was taxed with almost every conceivable political crime against the working class, ranging from acting as a 'propagandist of the peace mission of capitalism' to 'political cowardice'.[5] In this way the party paid its farewell to a man who had been a member of its leadership since the foundation and who for fourteen years had played a prominent part in the affairs of both the Comintern and the Profintern.

★   ★   ★

[1] *DW*, 5 Nov. 1931.   [2] Murphy, *New Horizons*, p. 298.
[3] *Communist Review*, iv, 167.
[4] Murphy to Politburo, 8 May 1932, printed in his *New Horizons*, pp. 302-4.
[5] Politburo statement, *Inprecorr*, xii, 409.

Gradually, however, and at first almost imperceptibly, the Comintern 'line' began to swing back towards a more effective policy. At the Eighth Session of the Central Council of the Profintern in December 1931 emphasis was placed once more on the need for work in the ordinary trade-union branches. Emmerich himself admitted that

> We in the R.I.L.U. are not altogether blameless if the revolutionary work within the reformist trade unions took a step backward in the most important capitalist countries since the Fifth Congress.

He did not hesitate, however, to throw the bulk of the blame on the national parties:

> We did not come to understand with sufficient rapidity the distortion of the line of the Fifth Congress in the individual sections, and did not liquidate and rectify these deviations quickly enough.[1]

Pollitt, who was attending the meeting, at once pointed out that, on the contrary, the 'individual sections' had got their 'distortion' from the statements of the Moscow secretariat:

> In England and other countries there has been a tendency for liquidation of work in the reformist trade unions, because there has been an impression, whatever may have been in the resolution, that work in the reformist trade unions did not matter, and a drive to carry out this work has not been carried out by the R.I.L.U. Executive Bureau, and certainly not by the international propaganda committees associated with the R.I.L.U.[2]

At all events, it was now generally accepted that the 'line' of complete independence from existing working-class organisations had to be abandoned. There was to be no more talk of founding new unions under Communist control, though the existing pair, the United Mineworkers of Scotland and the United Clothing Workers, were to be retained. The structure of the Minority Movement, which indeed was in a very brittle state, began to come in for criticism, and emphasis was placed on the need for supporting spontaneous rank-and-file movements in the unions, however these might differ in character from trade to trade.[3] It was typical, however, of the subordination of the whole

[1] *RILU Magazine*, 1 Feb. 1932, p. 65.   [2] *Ibid.*, p. 69.   [3] *Ibid.*, p. 66.

Profintern to the strategic interests of the Soviet Union, that plans for a new seamen's union were allowed to go ahead in spite of strong protests from the British delegation. Pollitt even went so far as to say that it would be a 'crime' if a new seamen's union were at once launched, as there were only 2,000 Minority Movement supporters out of 146,000 British seamen, and about two-thirds of the 2,000 were unemployed.[1] The National Union of Seamen had usually been regarded as one of the most right-wing of British trade unions, but as Pollitt pointed out it had at least re-affiliated to the T.U.C. and had thus come into line with the other unions.

Nevertheless, the plans went ahead, for the Russians were anxious above all to prevent the shipment of munitions to Japan, which seemed to be threatening their strategic interests in the Far East. The International of Seamen and Harbour Workers, a Profintern subsidiary with headquarters in Hamburg, was in charge of the arrangements, and it transferred considerable subsidies to London, where George Hardy, a former 'Wobbly', was in charge.[2] The International controlled a number of seamen's clubs throughout the world, which acted as its recruiting stations, and which appear to have offered all the more worldly attractions in order to sugar the Communist pill.[3] There were also some English-language journals, the *International Transport Worker* in particular, the publication of which in Britain was subsidised from Hamburg. Special efforts were made to recruit the foreign seamen who worked on British ships: agents were at work, for instance, among the coloured seamen at Cardiff and the Arabs who frequented South Shields, and occasional ugly disturbances took place at these ports.[4] But the whole attempt to form a new

[1] At the Eighth Session of the RILU Central Council, reported in *RILU Magazine*, 1 Feb. 1932, p. 70.

[2] *Seaman*, 30 Dec. 1931; G. Hardy, *Those Stormy Years* (1956), pp. 214-23.

[3] An advertisement of the clubs in the *International Transport Worker* of Jan-Feb. 1929 read: 'The missions cannot give the seaman the things he needs, owing to their policy of class distinction, rigid discipline with the "Almighty" hovering and watching. The only real place where the seaman can have a real healthy time is in the International Seamen's Clubs in all the ports where they exist.'

[4] *Seaman*, 3 Dec. 1930.

union in 1932, when unemployment was at its height, could not
but be disastrous. In the summer Jan Valtin, a German seaman
who served as a Comintern agent, was sent to England to
'liquidate' the affair.[1] George Hardy, who seems to have misled
the Profintern Secretariat about the prospects, was packed off to
Moscow to give an explanation of his failure.[2]

The campaign for the new seamen's union, however, had been
an exceptional case: in the course of 1932 the general policy involved a revival, albeit in a somewhat tentative fashion, of the
'united front' tactic. This did not mean collaboration with the
Labour Party, or with non-Communist trade union leaders: on
the contrary, Social-Democracy was still described as 'Social
Fascism', and there was no thought even in Germany that a
common front against the real Fascist threat was either necessary
or desirable. The furthest that the Communists were prepared to
go was to advocate the 'united front from below', which in
Britain meant attempting to win the local organisations of trade
unionism for their policy, and so securing a base of operations
against the existing union bureaucracy.[3]

It cannot be said that this switch of tactics gained any particular
successes while it was in operation, though any movement away
from the barren 'Class Against Class' policy was likely to halt the
decline in the party's industrial influence. The immediate result,
as it turned out, was the almost complete collapse of the tottering
Minority Movement, for many of the British Communists, overburdened with party duties as they were, regarded the Eighth
Session decisions as licence to abandon this increasingly sterile type
of work and return to activity in the existing unions. Willie Allan
described the lamentable situation:

From the centre of the Minority Movement right down to the
weakest group, this process of liquidation was clearly expressed,
with Secretariat and Executive Bureau of the Minority Movement

[1] Valtin, *Out of the Night*, pp. 328f.
[2] See his speech in Moscow reported in *RILU Magazine*, 1 Feb. 1932, pp. 70f.
[3] See Central Committee resolution of January 1932, published in *Communist Review*, iv, 55-69.

not being called together for several months, the district bureau
going out of existence, and many of the groups collapsing.[1]

There was a period of hesitation in the leadership as to what
should be done about the Minority Movement, but meanwhile
the problem was solving itself, and by the time the decision was
made, apparently in 1933, to bury the Movement, there was in
fact nothing left to bury. The industrial members of the party
now busied themselves with such unofficial bodies as the Members
Rights Movement in the A.E.U. and the Builders Forward Movement: and instead of seeking to recruit members of the Minority
Movement, and thus duplicating the organisation of the party on
a national basis, they now sought directly to win new members
for the party. In January 1932 it had been decided to concentrate
recruiting activity on the four principal industrial districts –
London, Scotland, Lancashire and South Wales – and special
attention was paid to selected factories and trade unions.[2] It was
difficult, however, to make much progress when sixty per cent of
the party's total membership was unemployed; and at the end of
the year there were only 200 employed miners in the party, only
150 employed textile workers, and, in the woollen textile industry of Yorkshire, only eight party members in the mills. The
total number of party members organised in 'factory cells', in
accordance with accepted Comintern procedure, was only 550,
the 'cells' themselves numbering 82.[3]

It thus remained a poor outlook for the British party, which
could muster such a small membership at a time when the
capitalist system seemed to be in its direst straits. Indirectly, however, events abroad, although unwelcome, were to come to the
rescue of the struggling C.P.G.B.: on 30th January 1933 Hitler
came into power in Germany, and at once began the systematic
destruction of the German working-class organisations, including
both the Social-Democratic Party (the so-called 'Social Fascists')
and the Communist Party – until then, the proudest and strongest
of the Communist Parties of the Western world.

---

[1] *Communist Review*, iv, 475.   [2] *Ibid.*, iv, 66.
[3] *Ibid.*, iv, 578f.

R. PALME DUTT

CHAPTER V

THE RED DECADE:
ENTRY OF THE INTELLECTUALS

THE triumph of Nazism in Germany was an important landmark
for the Comintern, and caused radical changes, not only in its
tactics but also in its internal balance of power. The destruction
of the open apparatus of the German Communist Party, and its
almost complete failure as an illegal organisation, still further
reduced the value of the remaining Western European parties in
the eyes of Stalin and his closest colleagues, at a time when the
success of the first Five Year Plan was in any case making the
Russian leaders feel more independent of the rest of the world.
The Comintern's status *vis-à-vis* the party of the Soviet Union
was thus weakened, both by National Socialism in Germany,
and by 'Socialism in One Country' in Russia. The predominance
of the interests of the Soviet leaders in the decisions of the Comintern was now guaranteed more effectively than before by the
increased proportion of Moscow-domiciled foreign exiles on its
executive.

In the new circumstances the Soviet foreign office pursued an
increasingly vigorous and flexible course of action. The subordination of the Comintern was shown by the way in which it
was induced to follow the twists of Soviet diplomacy, though
without having any foreknowledge of them. Stalin's attitude to
the Comintern, which he had always regarded with suspicion,
was shown in his willingness to sacrifice its interests if they clashed
with his national *realpolitik*. In order to allay the fears of the
existing governments of Britain and France and to prepare them
for an alliance with the Soviet, he relaxed the Comintern's detailed supervision of its national sections, secure in the knowledge
that groups of his own tried henchmen were in control of each of
them. The Profintern was quietly buried: the practice of sub-

sidising Comintern activities in the West, which was always strongly resented by the governments of the countries concerned, was severely curtailed if not altogether terminated; and, to the distress of many a coloured sympathiser, even the League Against Imperialism was relegated to a limbo of inactivity, for fear that it might embarrass the efforts of Soviet diplomacy to come to an understanding with the principal colonial powers. No propaganda organisation, however worthy its objects in terms of Marxist-Leninist philosophy, was permitted to function if it seemed likely to interfere with the achievement of short-term Russian objectives: the Proletarian Freethinkers International, for instance, disappeared as soon as the Soviet leaders had decided to ingratiate themselves with the Western powers, and its British section, the League of Socialist Freethinkers, which was only founded in 1933, was hastened to a death which appeared unduly sudden even for so sickly an infant – its membership was always exiguous.[1]

The relaxation of detailed executive control over the Comintern and the re-orientation of its activities was proclaimed at its Seventh World Congress in Moscow in 1935. This was the first Congress to be held since 1928, and the last ever to take place. The new policy was outlined in a resolution which declared:

> Taking into consideration the constantly growing importance and responsibility of the Communist Parties . . ., taking into consideration the necessity of concentrating operative leadership within the sections themselves, the Seventh World Congress instructs the E.C.C.I. . . . to proceed in deciding any question from the concrete situation and specific conditions obtaining in each particular country, and as a rule to avoid direct intervention in internal organisational matters of the Communist Parties.[2]

This resolution amounted to an admission of error in the past, by 'direct intervention' which presumably ignored the 'concrete situation'. But the past was not to be undone: there was no question of unseating the Stalinist cliques which had been imposed upon the national sections. Consequently, there could be

---

[1] For its inauguration (originally as 'The League of Militant Atheists') see *DW*, 19 Apr. 1933. Its journal, *The Fight*, appeared irregularly in 1934.
[2] ECCI, *Seventh Congress Report* (1936), Resolutions, p. 38.

no real danger of the lapsing of effective Russian control of the Communist Parties, even though their day-to-day activities were no longer to be supervised. Each country had its self-perpetuating group of obedient leaders who, like the Duke of Newcastle's bishops, could be expected to worship their maker. These leaders still made their pilgrimages to Moscow as before, though their trips were less frequently associated with the formal meetings of the International. And for those who stayed at home, a careful attention to Moscow foreign-language broadcasts would indicate the path of loyalty if, as all too often happened, their knowledge of the dialectic failed to forecast it in advance.

★   ★   ★

These developments were in part the natural result of the consolidation of the Russian Revolution into a national dictatorship. In such circumstances, as in France under Napoleon, ideological aims were subordinated to national interests or indeed to the interests of the autocrat himself, and only those who were furthest away from the centre of power were deceived by the lip-service still paid to abandoned principles. The transformation was a gradual one, although the tempo of the change was increased by the sudden success of Nazism in Germany. For some months of 1933 the Russian leaders were misled into thinking that friendly relations of the German and Russian military commanders could continue, and that Nazism would soon disappear, either as a result of a military coup or through failure to secure popular support. The German Communists had been under the impression that Hitler had only to be saddled with the responsibilities of government in order to be discredited, and that then the way would be clear for their own achievement of power. Only gradually did it transpire that these expectations were false, and that the Nazis had succeeded in destroying the effective strength of the German Communist Party, including its illegal organisation. In the meantime, at least until 1934, the official Russian attitude to the new Germany was equivocal.[1]

[1] E. H. Carr, *German-Soviet Relations Between the Two World Wars* (1952), pp. 109f.

Consequently, it was by several stages, rather than by a sudden complete switch, that the full 'popular front' tactic was developed for the use of the Communist Parties. The first stage, although it came as early as March 1933, was limited in its scope: the Comintern Executive instructed its national sections to approach the central organisations of the parties of the Second International with proposals for joint action; and in the meantime the sections were to 'refrain from making attacks on Social-Democratic organisations'.[1] This was a distinct step forward from the earlier 'united front from below', which had allowed no suspension of hostilities with the Social-Democratic leaders; but there was still no indication, if the attitude of the Social-Democratic leaders was unfavourable, that the suspension of hostilities would be turned into a deliberate courtship. At any rate, within three days of the receipt of the instructions from Moscow the obedient C.P.G.B. had shot off messages to the executives of the Labour Party, the I.L.P., the T.U.C. and the Co-operative Party inviting them to consider plans for joint activity.[2]

For many years the Communists had been doing their best to denigrate the existing leadership of the T.U.C. and the Labour Party, having been thwarted in the attempt to permeate the ranks of either. It was not surprising, therefore, that when faced by the new Communist proposals these two bodies should return an uncompromising negative and once more strengthen their precautions against infiltration. In any case, the sheer disparity of size between the Labour Party and the T.U.C. on the one hand, and the five or six thousand Communists on the other, made the idea of a 'united front' between these organisations seem ludicrous. In June 1933 the Labour Party issued a pamphlet entitled *The Communist Solar System*, which gave an outline of the now well-established Communist method of establishing and controlling subsidiary organisations; and in the same month the T.U.C. issued a circular to the unions dealing with this topic.[3] The Co-operative Party, although apparently less concerned about infiltration, also rejected the Communist invitation outright.

[1] *DW*, 8 Mar. 1933.   [2] *DW*, 11 Mar. 1933.
[3] T.U.C. *Report*, 1933, p. 174.

With the I.L.P., however, things were different. This party no longer retained the key importance in the working-class movement that it had had some thirty or even fifteen years earlier: the 1918 changes in the Labour Party constitution, allowing individual membership, had seen to that. In the course of the nineteen-twenties it gradually lost its position as the body most fully representative of British Socialism in general, and became a resort for critics of the Labour Party leadership. The process culminated in 1932, when the I.L.P. decided to disaffiliate altogether from the Labour Party. Although this led to a considerable loss of membership, the I.L.P. was in 1933-4 still at least as important as the Communist Party,[1] and the Communists realised that if they could 'capture' the I.L.P., or win over a substantial proportion of its members, they could immeasurably improve their own prospects of developing into a 'mass' organisation.

Inside the I.L.P. there was a group known as the Revolutionary Policy Committee which proposed a plan for 'sympathetic affiliation' to the Comintern. This group, which was led by Dr C. K. Cullen, an East London medical officer, and Jack Gaster, a Jewish solicitor, was in action at the I.L.P. Conference at Easter 1933: it carried a resolution, against the opposition of the party's executive, calling for negotiations to 'ascertain in what way the I.L.P. may assist in the work of the Communist International'.[2] This, however, was not quite what the C.P.G.B. itself wanted. Cullen and Gaster appeared to be attempting to turn the I.L.P. into the British section of the Comintern, maintaining that the C.P.G.B. had gone about things the wrong way. The leaders of the C.P.G.B on the other hand, expected the Revolutionary Policy Committee, if successful, to 'liquidate' the I.L.P. and to bring its members into the true 'British section' of the Comintern. This difference of aim caused friction: in 1934 the *Daily Worker* published an article which complained:

The leaders of the R.P.C. are comrades who privately agree with

[1] Detailed figures were not published, but Mr Francis Johnson, who was then the Financial Secretary, has kindly informed me that membership amounted to 16,773 in 1932, 11,092 in 1933, 7,166 in 1934 and 4,392 in 1935.

[2] *New Leader*, 21 Apr. 1933.

the programme of the Communist International, but who believe that the leading comrades of the C.P.G.B. do not understand 'tactics'. ... Precisely because of their 'tactical line' they have been out-manoeuvred time and time again by the more expert Parliamentary tacticians, Brockway and Maxton.[1]

It is true enough that the 1933 resolution had restored the initiative to the official leadership, led by Brockway and Maxton, in the very process of overriding their views: for the negotiations with the Comintern were left in their hands. There followed an elaborate public correspondence with Moscow, in the course of which the Comintern tried to split the I.L.P. by denouncing its 'reformist' leadership while appealing to its 'revolutionary' membership; while the I.L.P. executive led by Brockway, who was its chairman, sought to expose the Russian control of the International, and demanded various democratic safeguards. Brockway had lately been in America, where he had met Jay Lovestone, whose faction had been unconstitutionally ejected from control of the American C.P. in 1929 by orders of the International and, as we have seen, with the assistance of Harry Pollitt. Lovestone's analysis of the failings of the Comintern was evidently the basis of the case made by the I.L.P. leaders in these letters, justifying their request for guarantees.[2] When it is recalled that the I.L.P. now had a reputation for extreme Socialism of a strongly emotional type, the frankness and realism of its observations about the Comintern is striking:

> Its executives have assumed an increasingly detailed control of the operations of the national sections, and have narrowly circumscribed the latter's power of initiative. The desires of national sections have been overridden, their policies reversed by instructions from the centre, their leaders removed from office against the wishes of their members, or expelled from the party, and whole parties forced out of the C.I. In consequence, the C.I. has been split in country after country, its growth retarded and its members reduced. While the

[1] DW, 12 Feb. 1934. For a reply on behalf of the R.P.C., see the cyclostyled 'London R.P.C. Bulletin', March 1934, p. 3.
[2] A. F. Brockway, Inside the Left (1942), p. 233; Communist Party U.S.A. (Opposition), For Unity of the World Communist Movement: A letter to the I.L.P. of Great Britain (New York, 1934).

prestige of Soviet Russia has steadily risen, and whilst Soviet Russia has gained increasing support from the workers of other countries, the recent history of the sections of the C.I. in most countries has been one of continuous fission, their prestige is lower than in 1920, and their powers less than in 1923.[1]

According to the I.L.P. executive, the trouble lay in 'the effective control of the E.C.C.I. by the Communist Party of the Soviet Union'. This had led to a failure to understand the problems of different countries, to the 'mechanical transference' of Russian attitudes and problems to the Comintern as a whole, and to the 'deliberate policy of sacrificing the revolutionary movement' to the interests of the U.S.S.R. The remedies for these faults could only be found in reform of the Comintern, first, by extending the right of criticism among its members; secondly, by 'the preparation of important decisions of the C.I. through international discussions'; and thirdly, by the creation of 'a real collective international leadership based upon party representatives who are in the position to pass their own judgment upon the class relations in their countries'.[2]

This devastating analysis, which failed to provoke any adequate reply from Moscow, was not lost upon the rank and file of the I.L.P., some of whom were in any case alienated by the attempt of the Soviet Government to find a *modus vivendi* with the Nazis in 1933-4. The result was that at the annual conference of the I.L.P. at Easter 1934 the policy of 'sympathetic affiliation' was defeated by 98 votes to 51; and the 'day to day' co-operation with the C.P.G.B., which the I.L.P. had been operating for a year, was abandoned in favour of only limited joint activity for specific issues.[3] This may have slowed down, but certainly did not halt, the disintegration of the I.L.P., which had been rapidly losing members to the Labour Party as a result of collaboration with the Communists.

*　　*　　*

But if the Communists made comparatively little progress in

[1] *Communist International*, xi (1934), 258.　　　　[2] *Ibid.*, p. 260.
[3] *New Leader*, 6 Apr. 1934.

the sphere of their principal interest and efforts – the working-class movement as a whole – there were compensating advances elsewhere. Suddenly after Hitler's rise to power Communism became fashionable among the young, and especially among students and intellectuals. Their conversion was secured, not by the crude propaganda of the tiny British party, but by the apparent logic of international events, combined with feelings of social guilt thrust upon them by the depression. They were impressed especially by the success of the first Five Year Plan in Russia, and they readily accepted the view that only the methods of the Comintern could provide effective resistance to Fascism.

The C.P.G.B. of the later nineteen-twenties had had only a tiny smattering of intellectuals in its ranks; and the pioneers of party activity among the new generation at the universities appear to have picked up their faith on the continent, rather than at home. At Cambridge, for instance, David Guest, a young mathematician whose father had been a Labour M.P., had initiated activities on his return from a visit to Germany in 1931.[1] The most gifted writers of this generation developed an interest in social and political issues, and some of them, such as Christopher Isherwood and Stephen Spender, went off to Germany to study the death-throes of the Weimar Republic.[2] Soon it became clear that a whole school of new poets, including W. H. Auden, Cecil Day Lewis and Stephen Spender, could be distinguished from their predecessors as much as anything by their inclination to Marxism. In 1934 came the foundation of the *Left Review* under the auspices of a new body called the British Section of the Writers' International, a Communist-controlled body with headquarters in Moscow.[3]

The most striking feature of the *Left Review* was that its best contributors were all very young. There were among them a few members of the Communist Party of the nineteen-twenties, such as Tom Wintringham, who had been one of the twelve defen-

---

[1] C. Haden Guest (ed.), *David Guest: A Memoir* (1939), p. 89.
[2] S. Spender, *World Within World* (1951), pp. 129-38.
[3] *Left Review*, October 1934, p. 38. The parent body was really called the International Union of Revolutionary Writers.

dants in the 1925 Communist trial, and Ralph Fox, who had been working in the Comintern headquarters in Moscow at about the same time; but these were not the ablest or the most distinctive writers in the group. Those who had most to offer were still in their twenties or very early thirties – such as Day Lewis, whose poem 'The Communist' appeared in the second issue:

He is what your sons will be, the road these times must take.[1]

or such as Auden and Isherwood, the opening chorus of whose *Dog Beneath the Skin* was published in the number for May 1935.

Nor was it only the literary intellectuals who were attracted by Communism. 'Technocracy' was in the air in the middle nineteen-thirties, and scientists and engineers were readily attracted by the apparent devotion of the Soviet leaders to this concept. The chaos and waste of the capitalist countries during the depression were contrasted with the Soviet system of organising the rapid development of natural resources, and the latter naturally appealed most strongly to those with least insight into the political difficulties, but readiest appreciation of the technical advantages, of planning the resources and manpower of a great nation. A lead was provided by the veterans of Fabianism, the Webbs, Bernard Shaw, and H. G. Wells, who all hastened to pay their respects to Stalinism in these years. The Webbs were sufficiently misled by appearances to mistake the Stalinist dictatorship for the expression of the General Will: their well-known work, *Soviet Communism: A New Civilization?* first appeared in 1935; and a second edition, with the questionmark significantly omitted, appeared in 1937. Where these high authorities of political science pointed the way the devotees of natural and applied science readily entered in, and by 1937, when it was decided to found a magazine devoted to problems of Marxist theory – the *Modern Quarterly* – no less than five Fellows of the Royal Society could be found to sponsor it by serving on the Editorial Council.

All these intellectuals, with their leadership of literary lions and research scientists, formed a strange contrast to the older membership of the party, the proletarian sectaries whose Calvinistic

[1] *Ibid.*, Nov. 1934, p. 35.

fanaticism had survived the setbacks of the 'third period'. One obvious tie between the old and new memberships, however, was provided by the presence in both groups of a high proportion of Jews. In the early years of the party it had been the anti-semitism of the Czarist régime which had attracted Jews to the support of the Russian Revolution; now it was the anti-semitism of Nazi Germany which impelled them to rally to the cause which seemed to be most bitterly opposed to Fascism. It was not difficult for them to accept the view that the Soviet Union had solved its Jewish problem: many of the Russian revolutionaries, including the foreign minister of the middle nineteen-thirties, Maxim Litvinov, were of Jewish origin; and there were plenty of apologists of the Soviet Union among British Jewry, the most prominent of them being perhaps Andrew Rothstein, whose father had held high office in the Soviet diplomatic service. Rothstein under the pseudonym of 'R. F. Andrews' published a pamphlet for the C.P.G.B. with the title *What Lenin Said About the Jews*, in which he asked the rhetorical question

> In all the centuries of persecution of the Jews – until the civilised savages known as 'Nazis' appeared in Germany – has there ever been any blacker record than that of Russian Tzarism?[1]

With the aid of apologists like Rothstein, the continued existence of anti-semitism in Russia was to go unnoticed in left-wing circles until, in the final stages of the Stalinist era, it became impossible to conceal.

A further incentive to the growth of the party among the young, and especially among the Jewish population, was provided by the sudden rise in 1934 of the British Union of Fascists, led by Sir Oswald Mosley. Deriving much of his tactics and organisation from the German Nazis, as well as a certain *éclat* from the triumph of Hitler in 1933, Mosley made rapid progress, and temporarily secured the help of the *Daily Mail* and certain other organs of the press. In June 1934 he was able to stage a great demonstration at Olympia in London, the principal novel features

[1] 'R. F. Andrews' (A. F. Rothstein) (ed.), *What Lenin Said About the Jews* (1933, p. 1.)

of which were the elaborate spotlighting of the 'leader' and the brutal treatment of hecklers. The Fascists drew their supporters from all classes, and there was a significant proportion of former rank-and-file Communists among them, including two or three who became prospective parliamentary candidates.[1] But their unconcealed anti-semitism and their provocative marches through East London were bitterly resisted by the loyal members of the C.P.G.B., who were prepared to match disorder with disorder, and so acquired the reputation of being the stoutest opponents of Fascism. The Jewish population of the East End rallied to the party in fair numbers, one of the first to join after the Olympia meeting being Phil Piratin, later the Communist M.P. for Mile End.[2] But the disorders in the East End went on throughout 1935 and 1936, and only in 1937 did it become clearly evident that Fascism, in Britain at least, was in decline.

* * *

Thus the rise of Fascism on the continent and at home brought a corresponding prosperity to the C.P.G.B., and to its 'satellite' organisations – or at least to those of them that it chose to keep alive or to initiate afresh. The new recruits to the party were often fairly well off, and could provide generous subventions; a high proportion were very young and active men and women, whose efforts soon transformed the shaky Young Communist League into a national movement of some strength. Early in 1934 the I.L.P. Guild of Youth, which was almost autonomous, decided to accept the policy of 'sympathetic affiliation' to the Comintern which its parent organisation had rejected.[3] A few months later the I.L.P. executive took over its erring youth section again, but this led to a split among its members, many of whom seceded and joined the Y.C.L., thus providing the latter with an extra impetus.[4] Already by the beginning of 1935 the membership of the Y.C.L. had risen to over two thousand, which was three

[1] See brief biographies of ex-Communist Fascists in *Action*, 21 Nov. and 5 Dec. 1936, 20 Mar. 1937, 14 May 1938.
[2] P. Piratin, *Our Flag Stays Red* (1948), p. 5.
[3] *New Leader*, 25 May 1934.   [4] *DW*, 20 June 1935.

times the figure of a year before[1]; and a few months later it was able to begin a fortnightly paper of its own.

At the same time, the growth of Marxism among the intellectuals set up a great demand for left-wing political books and pamphlets. The Communist Party's literature department entered a period of unprecedented prosperity, and to meet the demand two small publishing firms run by sympathisers, Martin Lawrence Ltd. and Messrs Wishart, were amalgamated in 1936 into 'Lawrence and Wishart' and placed at the disposal of the party. Meanwhile members of the party who took an interest in bookselling had begun to find a ready scope for 'progressive' bookshops: one of the most successful was Collet's of Charing Cross Road, established by Eva Collet Reckitt, who had inherited a good deal of money from her family, the manufacturers of 'Reckitt's Blue'.[2] In the general prosperity, the circulation of established Communist organs began to expand: Dutt's *Labour Monthly*, for instance, was selling 6,500 copies in 1936, as against 4,500 in 1934, and its accumulated debt was gradually being paid off.[3]

The membership of the party itself shared this upward movement: it stood at less than 6,000 at the beginning of 1935, but by the time of the Comintern Congress in July it reached 7,700.[4] These gains in membership were by no means uniform throughout the country, and – what seemed more serious to the leaders of the party – there was little progress among the industrial workers to correspond to that among the intellectuals. This was due in part to the determined opposition of the General Council of the T.U.C., whose so-called 'Black Circular' of October 1934 forbade the trades councils to accept Communists as delegates, and urged the unions to exclude them from office.[5] It was true, of course, that the gradual reduction of unemployment tended to increase the proportion of party members who were actively engaged in industry; but it was only in South Wales that the party was able to get a real foothold in the unions. The old Communist 'break-

---

[1] *Inprecorr*, xv, 1281.   [2] M. B. Reckitt, *As It Happened* (1941), p. 249.
[3] *Labour Monthly*, xvi, 515 and xviii, 323.
[4] *Inprecorr*, xv, 1053.
[5] T.U.C. *Report* 1935, pp. 111f. for full text.

away' unions, the United Clothing Workers in London and the United Mineworkers of Scotland, were in the doldrums, and the party decided to cut its losses on these two bodies 'in the interests of unity': both of them went out of existence at the end of 1935, their members rejoining the older unions from which they had originally revolted.[1]

The political pattern of South Wales often differs considerably from that of the rest of Great Britain. It was evident that the Welsh miners, full of bitterness owing to their treatment by successive governments, were quite willing to accept the policy of the 'united front'. Mass demonstrations took place in South Wales early in 1935 when new regulations for a means test for unemployment benefits came into force: and from this campaign the Communist Party gained numerous recruits, its district membership being trebled in the six months ending in April.[2] In the course of the year no less than sixteen Communists were serving as local councillors in South Wales.[3] In 1936 Arthur Horner, whose tribulations during the 'third period' we have already traced, was elected President of the South Wales Miners Federation.[4] This, perhaps the most spectacular success of the new 'united front' tactic, must have led him to reflect somewhat wryly upon the twists of party policy in the preceding decade.

In other provincial districts, however, the party fared much less well. Lancashire, for example, had always been an unsatisfactory area for Communist propaganda – probably owing to the strength of Catholic and Orange sympathies among the workers. Indeed, if any totalitarian creed stood a chance of adoption by the Lancashire workers, it was likely to be Fascism.[5] This fact was well appreciated both in King Street and in the British Union headquarters in Chelsea: and the Duchy became an area of conflict between the two minority groups second only to London.[6] The Fascist policy for the cotton industry was a simple one: to

[1] Arnot, *Scottish Miners*, p. 222; Lerner, 'History of the United Clothing Workers Union', p. 434.
[2] *DW*, 22 Apr. 1935.   [3] *Inprecorr*, xv, 430.   [4] *DW*, 25 May 1936.
[5] Margaret McCarthy records that at Accrington a group of party members went over to Fascism *en bloc*. See her *Generation in Revolt*, p. 239.
[6] See R. Bishop, 'Fascist Concentration in Lancashire', *Inprecorr*, xv, 9.

resume control of the Indian fiscal system, so as to secure a guaranteed market for British exports. The Communist policy of nationalisation and planning seemed somehow less realistic. William Rust, who had been the first editor of the *Daily Worker*, was sent at the end of 1932 to assume the key post of district organiser in Manchester; and if anyone could have established the party's influence in the area, it was this tough and able young leader – although he was a Cockney. But it was an uphill struggle: the existing membership that he found on his arrival was lax in the payment of dues, slow to keep contact with headquarters, and sadly out of touch with the miners and cotton workers.[1]

Elsewhere, too, progress was gradual, except in London. Here a fairly large proportion of the intellectuals were concentrated, and as we have seen rapid recruiting took place in the Jewish districts of the East End. There were also certain groups of workers with special grievances who responded to the new technique of supporting independent rank-and-file movements in the unions. Notable successes, for instance, were gained in the London Busmen's Rank and File Movement, which was a revolt against the somewhat remote leadership provided for the busmen by the Transport and General Workers Union.[2] It was in this campaign that Bert Papworth first came to the fore as an agitator of considerable skill. By 1937 there was so much friction between the London busmen and the official leadership of their union that a 'break-away' union was actually established without Communist initiative.[3] The Communists could certainly have won control of this body if they had wished, but it was now their policy in the Transport and General Workers, as in the trade-union movement generally, to 'strengthen the union and change the executive'. They therefore concentrated, successfully in the long run, on obtaining positions of influence in the larger and older body. For the time being, however, progress was slow: it seemed that in most areas the party had to go through a period of probation with its 'united front' tactic before it could expect the workers

[1] *Communist Review*, vii, 57.
[2] H. A. Clegg, *Labour Relations in London Transport* (Oxford, 1950), pp. 103-38.   [3] *Ibid.*, p. 128.

to have forgotten the bad old days of sectarianism which had preceded it.

★　　★　　★

In the summer of 1935 the Seventh World Congress of the Comintern was held – an event which seemed to be more of a demonstration of anti-fascist and pro-Soviet solidarity than a serious discussion of political problems. So far as the British party was concerned, however, it was important that, as we have seen, the Congress declared for the relaxation of the tight and detailed control previously exerted by the Comintern and Profintern Secretariats. This did not result in any changes in the leadership of the British party, for there was no suggestion that the Stalinists should abdicate their positions just because their policies had been reversed. The declaration of non-intervention by the Comintern was evidently designed to propitiate Western opinion, not least among the parties of the Left: but coming when it did, after the U.S.S.R. had signed a pact of mutual assistance with France, it cut little ice with the I.L.P. at least, which was strongly pacifist in sentiment.

The Comintern Congress resulted in an intensification of the 'united front' tactic, which was now extended more fully by the British party in the political sphere. When a General Election took place in November 1935 the party rather ostentatiously withdrew all its candidates except two, and promised to support the Labour Party everywhere else.[1] This action provoked the secession of the Revolutionary Policy Committee from the I.L.P., which refused to do likewise; but the Committee had lost most of its following, and its action in joining the Communist Party cannot have brought over more than a few dozen supporters.[2] In any case, the Communist gesture brought no corresponding concession from the Labour Party, and the two Communist candidates had to fight against official Labour opposition. Harry Pollitt put up for East Rhondda, and secured a highly creditable poll (38 per cent of the total vote), which showed the strength of the party in South Wales; Willie Gallacher stood for West Fife, and with the aid of

[1] *DW*, 19 Oct. 1935.　[2] *Inprecorr*, xv, 1457f.; *New Leader*, 15 Nov. 1935.

the credit won by the sacrifice of the United Mineworkers of Scotland, he succeeded in defeating the sitting member, William Adamson, who had for long been the secretary of the rival union, the Scottish Mineworkers Union. Gallacher thus became the first Communist Member of Parliament since the defeat of Saklatvala in 1929.

As soon as the General Election was over, the C.P.G.B. applied to the Labour Party for affiliation – its first attempt since 1924.[1] The application was at once rejected by the Labour Party Executive, but the Communists launched a campaign to secure the reversal of the decision at the Labour Party Conference of the following year. The extent to which the Communists were now prepared to move away from their old sectarianism in pursuit of the hope of a 'united front' was shown by Pollitt's declaration, early in 1936, that the *Daily Worker* should be transformed

> . . . from a narrow party organ into the fighting daily newspaper of the united front. . . . Non-party people must be drawn on to the Editorial Board . . .[2]

There had indeed been an amazing transformation of policy since 1931. Few of the party's new recruits had any conception of the things it had been saying and doing only four or five years earlier. The Labour Party leaders, especially Herbert Morrison, still did their best to remind people of the Communists' transgressions in the past – of the subsidies they had received from Moscow, and of the switches of policy under instructions from the Comintern. A long manifesto on these lines, called *British Labour and Communism*, was published by the National Council of Labour in 1936.[3] But all this, in the face of Fascist aggression on the continent and the growth of Mosley's following at home, sounded remote and unimportant to the young. Stephen Spender has well expressed the standpoint of this new generation:

> Hitler forced politics on to non-political groups who suddenly became aware that they had interests in common. Not only the Jews, but also the intellectuals, because their position was directly attacked,

---

[1] Labour Party *Report*, 1936, pp. 50f.   [2] *Inprecorr*, xvi, 110.
[3] Printed in full in Labour Party *Report*, 1936, pp. 296-300.

and through sympathy with their colleagues who lived tormented under Fascism, acquired an intensity of vision and a fury in their non-political politics which the professional politicians did not share.[1]

They felt that the fight was on, and that they had to choose sides in a world-wide struggle. In joining the Communist Party they were joining an international army; they did not feel, and for the most part they did not expect to feel, that they themselves could exert any control over the discipline to which they were submitting themselves. Pollitt was their 'leader', just as Stalin was the leader of the Comintern as a whole and Hitler the leader of the Nazis. The 'cult of personality' was accepted as the best reply to Fascist propaganda, for it implied that Communists also could discipline themselves for battle. Congresses of the C.P.G.B., like those of the Comintern, became occasions for a parade of solidarity rather than for the sober discussion of policy. Pollitt was greeted with cheers and the singing of the 'Internationale': there could be no question of an internal challenge to his position, although the policy which he and Dutt had advocated at the time of their rise to power in 1929 had been turned completely upside down.

In fact, the Communist leadership was doing all it could to conceal its past from the new recruits that it had made. When in 1937 Tom Bell, one of the party's veterans, published an outline history of the party, recounting the sectarian past with a fair amount of detail, his work was at once denounced by the party executive as 'gravely unsatisfactory'[2]; and Allen Hutt, whose own *Post-War History of the British Working Class* represented the party's official line at this time, even suggested that 'A strong case can be made out against the whole conception of a separate History of the Communist Party at this stage'.[3] Hutt went so far as to describe Bell as 'a revolutionary sectarian who has never decisively broken with his evil old traditions' – a remark of brazen affrontery, for Bell had been one of those excluded from the party leadership in 1929 for his determined opposition to sectarianism. Hutt's own work, as may be imagined, had very

---

[1] Spender, *op. cit.*, p. 190. [2] *Labour Monthly*, xix, 453. [3] *Ibid.*, 382.

little to say about the party's policy in the period 1928-33, and omitted any reference to the role of the Comintern and the Profintern in those years. Thus the new members of the party were prevented from learning about its past, and few of them even discovered how the existing Politburo had become established. At the top, however, things remained much the same: the Stalinist group was in control, and the older members knew how it had got there; its tactics had changed, but its methods of formulating them, and its long-term aims, were the same as before.

CHAPTER VI

THE RED DECADE:
SPAIN AND THE PURGES

In 1936 the growth of the party, especially among intellectuals, received fresh impetus from the Spanish Civil War, which broke out in July. Spanish political struggles rarely have much immediate relevance for the rest of the world, but the rest of the world has often had difficulty in appreciating this fact. At a time when the democratic powers of Europe were facing the challenge of Nazism and Fascism, it seemed of vital importance that the new Spanish Republic should not succumb to a revolt engineered by a military clique and supported by Italian and German arms.

The role of Communism in Spain was at first a relatively minor one, although the partisans of General Franco's rebellion did not scruple to magnify it for propaganda purposes. The Spanish Communist Party at the beginning of the war was tiny beside the Socialists, the Anarcho-Syndicalists, the P.O.U.M., and other Republican groups.[1] But in September Stalin decided to provide the Spanish government with military support, and as a result the political situation quickly changed. The International Brigade of volunteers was formed under the auspices of the Comintern; supplies of armaments began to trickle in from the Soviet Union; and the youth of the government-controlled areas, to show its appreciation, flocked to the Spanish Communist Party. The hope of increased aid from Russia, combined with pressure from the Comintern, soon increased its weight in the Spanish Government.

Meanwhile the International Brigade had been recruiting its forces, and at first the great bulk of its members were Frenchmen, Germans or Italians. The Germans and Italians were exiles from

[1] D. T. Cattell, *Communism and the Spanish Civil War* (Berkeley, Calif., 1955), p. 31. A useful and judicious survey of a controversial subject.

their homes, mostly Communists, who were keen to make the most of their first opportunity to come to grips with Fascism on something like equal terms. Many of them were seasoned soldiers; and the first battalions of the brigade, ill-equipped though they were, played a large part in saving Madrid in the late months of 1936, as the columns of Franco's army closed in upon the capital from three sides.

The International Brigade was not officially Communist, but 'anti-fascist'; in fact, however, its organisation and control were the work of the Comintern, and each of the parties was instructed to provide recruits for it. In Britain it was therefore the C.P.G.B. which took charge of the registration and forwarding of volunteers. Even when, in January 1937, the British Government placed an embargo on volunteering for either side in the Civil War, the party continued to make the necessary arrangements for the flow of British reinforcements through a headquarters in Paris. The principal London agent of this movement was R. W. Robson, a 'tall, thin, dour man' who had once been London District organiser of the party; while in Paris Charlotte Haldane, the Jewish-American wife of the scientist J. B. S. Haldane, acted as staging officer for some time.[1] The recruits themselves contained a high proportion of members of the party or the Y.C.L., especially in the early months, but there was a fair number of Labour Party or I.L.P. members, as well as more than a smattering of recruits who, without any particular political interest, were either spoiling for a fight or simply preferred it to the monotony of unemployment.

It was as early as October 1936 that the first British volunteers in Spain were organised in the 'Tom Mann *Centuria*', which served on the Aragon front. There were also a few among the defenders of Madrid in November.[2] It was then decided to constitute a British Battalion of the International Brigade, and a contingent of company strength saw action on the Cordoba front at Christmas. The battalion which was built up early in 1937 became the nucleus of the XV Brigade, composed principally of British,

[1] C. Haldane, *Truth Will Out* (1949), pp. 100ff.
[2] See, for example, E. Romilly, *Boadilla* (1937).

American and Canadian volunteers.[1] The British Battalion was involved in very heavy fighting in 1937: in the defence of the Madrid-Valencia road, in February, it had some four hundred casualties, and in the Brunete offensive in July its remaining three hundred effectives were reduced at one point to forty-two. Reinforcements arrived later in the year, but the battalion was again heavily engaged early in 1938 in the attempt to stem the advance of Franco's troops on the Aragon front, and by April the strength was down to seventy. In July it was engaged in the Ebro counter-offensive; and in September it was once again in action at the moment when, by international agreement, the Spanish Government undertook to disband the brigade.

The commanders of the British units were quite often not Communists, and one of the companies was called the 'Major Attlee Company' as a compliment to the leader of the Labour Party. But the political commissars, who had special responsibilities for discipline, morale, and political instruction, were, it seems, invariably members of the Communist Party.[2] In this way the character of the International Brigade corresponded to that of many another 'satellite' organisation of the party: the effective control was in Communist hands, although the distribution of the highest offices suggested a variety of political standpoints. It became quite a routine matter for the British party to despatch some of its district organisers and other full-time officials for a tour of duty as political commissars in the battalion. Among those who served in this way were George Brown of Manchester and Walter Tapsell, the general manager of the *Daily Worker* (who were both killed), David Springhall of London, Peter Kerrigan of Glasgow, and Bert Williams of the Midlands District. Putting political leaders straight into military posts with disciplinary responsibilities was a risky expedient, and did not always prove successful: but considering the severity of the campaigns that the battalion underwent and the losses that it suffered, it is not surprising that some of the commissars occasionally showed signs

[1] See W. Rust, *Britons in Spain: the History of the British Battalion* (1939).
[2] On the role of the political commissars, see Hugh Slater in *Inprecorr*, xvi, 1516f.

of battle strain. The fighting itself brought to the fore a number
of natural leaders, many of whom had little loyalty to the party,
at least after the war was over. Some of these had had previous
military experience, such as Tom Wintringham, who commanded
the battalion for a time before being wounded[1]; and Fred Copeman, who had been discharged from the Navy for his part in the
Invergordon Mutiny.[2] 'Jock' Cunningham, who was described
by Pollitt as 'our British Chapayev'[3] (after the Russian guerilla
leader of the revolutionary period) actually resigned from the
party after a disagreement with the Politburo on how the battalion
should be run.[4]

The record of the British Battalion in Spain was not, of course,
all idealism and noble sacrifice, as the party press in Britain made
out. There was tension between the Communists and those non-
Communists who disliked the strictness of party control; there
were volunteers who, on grounds of democratic theory, resented
the privileges of the officers, and there were officers who exerted
their authority with unnecessary vigour. There were desertions,
there was malingering, there were cases of cowardice in the face
of the enemy. But by and large, the members of the British
Battalion deserved the admiration and support of the British
labour movement: they certainly got little else for their sacrifices
in the cause. As part of the Republican forces, they engaged in an
unequal struggle, and acquitted themselves well in tests that
would have tried the bravest and toughest of men. They were not
all idealists, but there were plenty of idealists among them; and
those who, sharing the same ideals, yet stayed at home, felt an
admiration for the International Brigade which was tinged with
a sense of personal guilt. Out of every ten Britons who served,
two were killed, and another four wounded; and of those who
died, over two hundred and fifty – that is to say, more than half –
were members of the Communist Party or of the Y.C.L.[5]

All this was excellent propaganda for the party. It was a little
alarming at times that so many of its best younger leaders were

[1] See his *English Captain* (1939).   [2] Copeman, *Reason in Revolt*, pp. 78ff.
[3] *DW*, 15 Mar. 1937.   [4] Copeman, *op. cit.*, p. 139.
[5] For an almost complete casualty list see Rust, *op. cit.*, pp. 189-99.

among the casualties. But all the same, the more casualties, the more honour to the party; and indeed for the Communists, as for the early Christians, the blood of the martyrs was the seed of the church. The whole of the labour movement and the intellectual Left was stirred by the sacrifice of young lives – men of obvious talent in various fields, such as Ralph Fox, the novelist, John Cornford, the young Cambridge undergraduate and poet, Clem Beckett, the speedway rider. The hesitant policy of the Labour Party and the T.U.C., and their continued opposition to proposals for a 'united front', seemed to stand in painful contrast to the manly behaviour of those who fought and died in Spain.

There were however some disquieting features of the war itself, which suggested that collaboration between Communists and other left-wing bodies did not work smoothly even in a war against Fascism. It was not merely the fact of effective Communist control over the International Brigade which worried people; it was rather the fact that the Brigade, and other forces controlled by the Communists, could be used against the other political groups in the Republican coalition, for the purpose of extending Communist influence at their expense. George Orwell, who fought on the Republican side in the Civil War, but not in the International Brigade, witnessed the Communist *coup* in Barcelona in May 1937, when the P.O.U.M., a dissident Marxist organisation, was suppressed and its leaders thrown into prison. He reported his findings to the I.L.P. in Britain, which regarded the P.O.U.M. as its 'sister' party in Spain, and he later recounted the story more fully in his *Homage to Catalonia*.[1]

Still, in the general enthusiasm for the Republican cause, such incidents were not widely noticed, and the I.L.P.'s concern seemed to many to be unduly moralistic. The *Daily Worker*'s own reporter, 'Frank Pitcairn' (Claud Cockburn, a former *Times* correspondent), gave a very different version of the events, and it was difficult to be sure of the truth. In any event, the important thing seemed to be to raise funds for the upkeep of the British Battalion and for assistance to the soldiers and civilians on the Republican

[1] Orwell, 'Eyewitness in Spain', *Controversy*, August 1937, pp. 85-8; *Homage to Catalonia* (1938).

side; and many people who were not Communists were prepared to co-operate wholeheartedly in this. Trade-union delegations and Labour members of Parliament visited the front to pledge their support; and at innumerable public meetings in Britain, the Republican case was put and the contributions came flowing in. It was no doubt the intellectuals who were most stirred by the Spanish War; but the labour movement as a whole was not far behind, and often an unopened pay packet was to be found among the gifts for 'Aid to Spain'.[1] No such enthusiasm for a foreign cause had been engendered in Britain since the 'stillness at Appomattox'.

*   *   *

It was just before the outbreak of the Spanish war that a new organ of left-wing propaganda made its appearance – an organ which swelled to surprising dimensions in the hot-house political atmosphere of the time. This was the Left Book Club, launched by Victor Gollancz, the publisher, as a means of establishing a large guaranteed sale for books of left-wing political interest, which could consequently be published very cheaply. The uniform orange, or later red, covers of these books are today to be seen in their dozens on the shelves of the second-hand bookshops, a reminder of the extent if not of the enduring quality of the whole enterprise. The monthly selection was chosen by a panel of three – Victor Gollancz himself, Harold Laski, the Labour Party's leading intellectual, and John Strachey. Of these three, only John Strachey was a 'Communist', and even he may never have been a member of the party in the technical sense, although he advised others to join.[2] However, the Left Book Club served the ends of the Communist Party very well, for although the books that it published were not all in accordance with the party 'line', a high proportion of them were, and manuscripts that seemed to express any undue criticism of the 'line', even if written from a left-wing standpoint, were omitted from the list of publications.[3]

---

[1] D. Hyde, *I Believed* (1951), p. 58.

[2] See his *Coming Struggle for Power* (4th ed., 1934), pp. 371ff.

[3] This happened with a work by August Thalheimer, who belonged to a group expelled from the German C.P. See *Controversy*, June 1937, p. 42.

It is difficult not to feel a certain respect for the skill with which the Communist Party made use of the Left Book Club, without ever having actual control over its operations. Victor Gollancz himself, who seems at first to have been only vaguely aware of what was going on, gave a very simple explanation in 1937 of how it was that so many books representing the party's attitude were being published by the club:

> At present Communists . . . *offer* us books: we have to rack our brains to invent books for Liberals, Trade Unionists, and Labour Party people to write – and then we have to find people to write them.[1]

What had happened, in short, was that the Communists had realised the value of the Club as a mass propaganda agency, and had taken steps to make sure that the propaganda was their own. This gave them access to a reading public of at least 50,000, which was the membership of the Club at the end of 1937.[2] Gollancz himself was soon getting perturbed by the extent to which the Club began to turn into a Communist 'satellite' organisation: some of the local groups of the Club, for instance, would devote their meeting time, not to a discussion of issues raised by the current volumes, but to direct political agitation such as chalking slogans in the streets.[3] By the end of 1938, with the Spanish War drawing to a close and fresh problems dividing the Communists from other left-wing groups, Gollancz confessed rather wistfully:

> I have allowed myself, I think . . . to become too much of a propagandist and too little of an educator. . . . Only by the *clash* of ideas does a mind become truly free.[4]

Gollancz's idea of the 'truly free mind' must have seemed a little puzzling to the Communist leaders who had obtained so many advantages from the Club: that had never been quite the way in which they were accustomed to look at things.

The success of the Left Book Club, however, was symptomatic of a widespread demand for some sort of unity among those who were awake to the menace of Fascism. It was natural, therefore,

[1] *Left News,* July 1937, p. 422. [2] *Ibid.,* Nov. 1937, p. 566.
[3] *Ibid.,* Nov. 1938, p. 1033. [4] *Ibid.,* p. 1035.

that in these years the Communists should make fresh efforts to secure their object of a 'united front'. Extra incentive was provided by the formation in the early summer of 1936 of a 'Popular Front' Government in France, under Leon Blum, the Socialist leader, and with Communist support. In Britain, the initiative was now taken by a new organisation of left-wingers inside the Labour Party, which was called the Socialist League. At the invitation of Sir Stafford Cripps, who was the most prominent member of the League, a series of discussions was held between the League itself, the I.L.P. and the Communist Party in an attempt to secure a basis for agreement between the three bodies. Fenner Brockway, who attended these meetings, has written of Pollitt's skill in 'wooing' Cripps for his own standpoint, with Dutt, like 'a Buddhist monk . . . secretive, suspicious, waiting and watching'.[1] The Communist proposal was that the I.L.P. and the Communist Party should both seek unconditional affiliation to the Labour Party, but the I.L.P., which had disaffiliated from the Labour Party only a few years earlier, refused at first to consider affiliation except under conditions such as the Labour Party was very unlikely to accept. In the end, a tenuous form of co-operation was agreed upon between all three bodies – sufficient at least to allow their leaders all to speak from the same platforms. But the campaign was killed by the opposition of the Labour Party Executive, which early in 1937 insisted on disaffiliating the Socialist League and declaring its members ineligible for membership of the Labour Party.[2] In the face of these strong measures Cripps and his colleagues decided to dissolve the Socialist League, and to carry on the fight for unity in an individual capacity.

Collaboration between the I.L.P. and the C.P.G.B. continued to some extent after the dissolution of the Socialist League, but it was restricted to joint action on specific issues, such as the grievances of the unemployed, and opposition to the British Union of Fascists.[3] Sir Stafford Cripps, George Strauss, Aneurin Bevan and other members of the Labour Party also continued to demand a 'Popular Front', but in 1938 the spirit seemed to go out of the

---

[1] Brockway, *Inside the Left*, p. 265.   [2] Labour Party *Report*, 1937, p. 27.
[3] Brockway, *op. cit.*, pp. 269f.

campaign, and early in 1939 the Labour Party Executive decided to expel the offenders – a drastic step which was confirmed by an overwhelming majority at the following party conference.[1]

The trouble was that basic disagreements on policy existed all along between the Communists and the other members of the Left, and a number of events took place in the period which considerably cooled the ardour of the non-Communist Left for any sort of 'Popular Front' when the temporary enthusiasm engendered by the Spanish War had begun to wear off. For one thing, the pacifists and the less opportunistic of the extreme Socialists were shocked by the Soviet policy of making military alliances with the 'capitalist' powers of Western Europe. Further to this, there were the stories that began to circulate, especially in 1938, about the behaviour of the Communists in Spain: Orwell's *Homage to Catalonia* was published early that year. And, even more important, there was the question of the 'treason trials' in Russia – a question which embarrassed the Communists and caused a good deal of heart-searching throughout the rest of the Left.

*   *   *

Much light has been thrown on what happened in Russia in the nineteen-thirties by the recent revelations by Krushchev at the Twentieth Congress of the Communist Party of the Soviet Union. We now know that after the assassination of Kirov in December 1934 Stalin's suspicions of his old revolutionary colleagues reached an extraordinary pitch of frenzy. It seems to have been his morbid fear of links with foreign country that accounted for the special concentration of his wrath upon old members of the Comintern leadership, Jews and military commanders who had had contacts with Germany. The names of the principal victims and the details of their trials were published at the time and caused great uneasiness: for even if the accusations against them were true, the extent of the alleged conspiracies was enough to alarm even the most trusting supporters of Stalin. Thus, for instance, of those who were elected to the Central Committee of the Communist Party of the Soviet Union at its Seventeenth

[1] Labour Party *Report*, 1939, pp. 43ff., 291ff.

Congress in 1934 no less than seventy per cent were shot, mostly in 1937-8.

The first of the great series of trials took place in 1936, the year of the promulgation of the new Soviet Constitution, 'the most democratic in the world'. Zinoviev, the former President of the Comintern, and Kamenev, another of Lenin's closest colleagues, were executed on this occasion. Then in 1937 came two major trials: that of Radek and Piatakov, among others, in January, and then the secret trial of Marshal Tukhachevsky and other generals in June. In March 1938 came the 'trial of the twenty-one', at which Yagoda, the former police chief (who had provided the evidence against Zinoviev and Kamenev), and Bukharin, a former Comintern leader, were condemned. The atmosphere of terror was, if anything, increased by the fact that those who were tried in public made a show of admitting their guilt and demanding the death penalty for themselves.

The leaders of the British Communist Party were well aware of the full extent of the Russian purges, which ran far beyond this list of the most prominent victims. Pollitt, for instance, must have been severely shaken by the disappearance of Rose Cohen, an old friend of his from London who had married the former Comintern agent in Britain, D. Petrovsky, and who now followed her husband into the obscurity of a Soviet prison.[1] When Pollitt and his colleagues visited Moscow, they sensed the change in the climate of discussion, and marked the absence of their old friends from the Comintern leadership. They themselves were fairly safe, for they had their British passports. But on their return to England, they did not speak out against the terror: on the contrary, they loudly justified the executions to their fellow-Communists and to the public. After the Zinoviev-Kamenev trial, the Central Committee of the C.P.G.B. declared its support for the Russian party in

> ... the measures taken against the Trotsky-Zinoviev terrorists, whose treacherous activities against the Workers' State have met with well-merited sentences of death.[2]

[1] *Militant*, Feb. 1938; Reckitt, *As it Happened*, pp. 148f.
[2] *Inprecorr*, xvi, 1092.

When Radek was tried and condemned, a C.P.G.B. statement declared:

> The evidence brought out at this trial has proved conclusively the terrible guilt of the Trotsky terrorists.[1]

And when the generals were shot, the British party's Central Committee decided to

> ... congratulate the workers and peasants of the Soviet Union, their party and their government on the drastic measures which they are taking to root out wreckers and spies from their midst.[2]

Nor did the British leaders falter in their comment as the trials went on, but rather the contrary. In March 1938, Pollitt could say:

> The trial of the twenty-one political and moral degenerates in Moscow is a mighty demonstration to the world of the power and strength of the Soviet Union.[3]

How was it that the British Communists, safe beyond the reach of Stalin's executioners, were able and willing to keep up this pretence? The answer is to be found at a variety of levels. The old leaders of the party, who had served the Comintern for so many years, had an infinite number of personal ties with Russia. Some of them had married Russians; others had relatives or close friends resident in the Soviet Union. If, in the safety of the British Isles, they were to speak out against the Stalinist terror, the certain result would be to place these relatives and friends among the victims of the next purge. But apart from this, we must take into account the mounting international tension of these years. World war seemed to be inevitable: in Spain indeed, the prelude was already being fought out. The Russian trials, even in their vast extent, could be made out to be justified by the extremity of the crisis. Necessity knows no law, especially for a Marxist, and the British Communists convinced themselves that Stalin had acted out of necessity. For propaganda purposes, they also made out that he had acted according to law.

[1] *DW*, 1 Feb. 1937.
[2] CP, *Report of Central Committee to 15th Congress* (1938), p. 53.
[3] *Inprecorr*, xviii, 309.

So far as the technical arguments were concerned, the party was well served by its legal advisers. D. N. Pritt, who at this time was a leading member of the Left wing of the Labour Party (he served on the Labour Party Executive from 1937 to 1940) had this to say of the Zinoviev trial:

> I was indeed impressed. The great new land . . . had shown me that it can build and maintain in the profession I understand, a fine system and a fine tradition.[1]

Another barrister who often worked for the Communist Party, Dudley Collard, attended the Radek trial in 1936, and wrote a book about it on his return. Collard went so far as to mention the theory that 'Stalin is engaged in polishing off all his old associates', but he concluded that this was a 'completely unscrupulous' suggestion and 'pure nonsense'. 'My own considered opinion', he said,

> formed and expressed as a lawyer, soberly and deliberately, is that the trial was conducted fairly and regularly according to the rules of procedure, that the defendants were fully guilty of the crimes charged against them, and that in the circumstances the sentence was a proper one.[2]

These certificates of legal propriety, issued by barristers of evident ability, went far to satisfy the troubled consciences of the rank and file of the party, especially in the prevailing conditions of 'inner party democracy', which now hardly extended to the serious discussion of political problems. Disagreements not infrequently took place between the Politburo and some of the lesser officials of the party, particularly if the latter were running 'satellite' organisations whose interests might conflict with those of the party. Hannington, for instance, was excluded from the Central Committee in 1938 for opposing the current 'line' on the National Unemployed Workers' Movement, which was so largely his own creation[3]; and, as we have seen, Cunningham left the party because of its treatment of the British Battalion. Then in

---

[1] *DW*, 3 Sept. 1936.
[2] D. Collard, *Soviet Justice and the Trial of Radek and Others* (1937), pp. 82, 105f.   [3] Copeman, *op. cit.*, pp. 153f.

1939 Copeman, who was managing the International Brigade Dependents' Aid Fund, broke away after a quarrel with his colleagues at King Street as to how its finances should be run.[1] But these matters were settled so far as possible in private, and were not thrashed out by the rank and file membership. The party, geared as it was to a quasi-military role in the existing political situation, treated each of its national congresses as an opportunity for a display of enthusiasm rather than as a forum for serious deliberation. Ian Mackay of the *News Chronicle*, reporting the Thirteenth Congress in 1935, had complained not unjustly of the dullness of the occasion, of the monotonously repeated singing of the 'Internationale', and of the general lack of opposition to the platform. 'Time was', he said, 'when a unanimous resolution at a Communist congress would have been as incongruous as a Primrose Dame in the chair. The party was alive then . . .'[2]

It was still laid down in the party's statutes, of course, that there should be discussion inside the party about the various political issues of the day. But the control of the party was vested, by means of the 'panel' system of election, in a self-perpetuating oligarchy, and this prevented the discussion from ever having any real significance: try as they might, the party leaders could not get it going. In 1936 a monthly journal called *Discussion* was started for this particular purpose, but the members of the party seemed to be unable to rise to the bait. Too many subjects were, either by editorial policy or by self-discipline of the membership, ruled out of order, and what was left was not enough to make the journal interesting. It petered out after a few months.

As we might expect, to find a journal in which such questions as the Russian trials and the internal conflicts of the Spanish Republican parties were seriously explored from different angles, we must turn to the press outside Communist control. C. A. Smith, then of the I.L.P., in 1936 founded a monthly called *Controversy*, and this for a brief period acted as a genuinely open forum of left-wing opinion, in which Communist propagandists were forced to argue their case seriously against the criticisms of

[1] *Ibid.*, pp. 178-80. [2] *News Chronicle*, 8 Feb. 1935.

other Socialists. Orwell's report on the situation in Catalonia was published in the issue for August 1937, and an anonymous writer contributed damning statistics on the effect of the purges on the old Bolshevik revolutionaries. But the rank and file of the Communist Party were not encouraged to read *Controversy*. Any criticisms of Soviet policy from the standpoint of the Left were instantly labelled 'Trotskyist', and, once so labelled, were regarded as beyond the need for further serious consideration.

★   ★   ★

It is probable, all the same, that these awkward issues slowed up the expansion of the party membership, which had gone ahead rapidly in the early months of the Spanish War. Although at the time of the formation of the International Brigade no less than five district organisers had been sent to Spain,[1] the year 1936 was notable for an expansion of party membership unequalled except in the crises of 1926 and 1931. From a total of about 7,500 early in that year, the figures rose rapidly to 11,500 in November.[2] Thereafter, however, in spite of most favourable conditions for recruitment, the expansion slowed down: it was 12,250 in May 1937, and 15,570 in September 1938.[3] In the first eight months of 1939 – after the withdrawal of the International Brigade from Spain – the party remained fairly constant in size with about 18,000 members. It was not without reason that Manuilsky complained in March 1939 that the British party was

> ... one of the most backward sections of the Comintern. It has not succeeded in breaking through to the main sections of the British working class.[4]

Moreover, what recruitment there was continued to be extremely uneven. In 1939 two-fifths of the membership total was in London, but recruiting in other industrial districts was sluggish, and the gains seemed to be largely confined to the intellectuals.[5] This situation was largely a reflection of the existing organisational

---

[1] *DW*, 27 May 1937.   [2] *Discussion*, Apr. 1936, p. 17; Nov. 1936, p. 12.
[3] *WNV*, xx, 415.   [4] *DW*, 17 Mar. 1939, reporting CPSU Congress.
[5] CP, *Report of Central Committee to 16th Congress* (1939), p. 13. This Congress, due to be held in October, did not meet.

structure of the labour movement. At the universities, the student
Socialist societies affiliated to the University Labour Federation
did not discriminate against Communists, who thus had a wide-
open field of propaganda among all university men and women
who were inclined towards the Left. In the trade unions, however,
the Communists had long been held in check by restrictions
dating from the nineteen-twenties, and as we have seen, the
General Council of the T.U.C. tightened its precautions in 1934
by the adoption of the so-called 'Black Circular'. As for the
Labour Party, Communists were excluded from membership,
and could only participate in its work by keeping their Communism secret.

It might perhaps be assumed that the intellectuals would be
the first to sense the grim reality of the Moscow trials, and the
readiest to declare their abhorrence. It often happens, however,
that the intellectual is more easily deceived about political matters
than the manual worker: indeed, if the truth be told, he is often
less rational than his professional role would suggest. Self-
deception was apparently more prevalent among them than any
cynical dissimulation of reality – at least, if we may accept as
genuine the astonishing flood of tortured self-criticism which
followed the Krushchev revelations of 1956. They took at face
value what they were told and saw on their carefully-shepherded
tours of the U.S.S.R., or what they read in *Russia Today*, the
journal of the Friends of the Soviet Union; and they really
believed that the healthy athletes whose photographs appeared
with monotonous repetition in the *Daily Worker* were typical of
the Russian population as a whole.

And so the number of intellectuals in the party continued to
increase, and by August 1939 must have been out of all proportion
to their strength in the country as a whole. It is difficult, however,
to be sure of the figures: those of them who had special distinction
or qualifications were often told to keep their party membership
secret, on the ground that they could do better work for the party
'from outside'. It was true enough, of course, that a supposed non-
Communist who advocated a particular line of policy was more
likely to be believed by most people than a Communist; and if

H

he belonged to another political party, he might well help in 'capturing' that party's organisation for the Communist Party. This sort of activity was especially common among the various youth organisations of the later nineteen-thirties, a surprising number of which appear to have succumbed to Communist control. Of the tendency of prominent intellectuals to serve the party in secret, we have many examples. Charlotte Haldane, for instance, was a member of the party from 1937, but she was told to keep this fact secret, and after doing various work for the Comintern in France, Spain and China, she entered the St Pancras Borough Council in 1940 as a Labour Party member.[1] Her husband, J. B. S. Haldane, also worked for the party as a 'crypto-Communist', and only openly identified himself with it in 1942.[2] Philip Toynbee, who was in the party as an Oxford undergraduate, has said of his own position:

> I was not a clandestine member of the party, but sat on the little iceberg peak above the submarine majority, revealing, as we used to say, 'the Face of the Party'.[3]

Douglas Hyde, later the news editor of the *Daily Worker*, has recounted the story of his own activities in a Labour Party in the London area. He gradually won over his leading colleagues until, one day, at a special meeting, he was able to bring them all together and announce, to the surprise of them all, that each and every one had become a secret Communist.[4] Many of these 'crypto-Communists' in the Labour Party were ordered to come out in their true colours in the summer of 1939, and for several weeks hardly a day passed without some official of a local Labour Party loudly proclaiming his conversion to Communism.

The ordinary rank-and-file member of the C.P.G.B. naturally did not know who the 'crypto-Communists' were, although he might have a shrewd idea of many of them. However, a 'Cadres Department' for the training of party leaders was developed in this period, and it appears that those in charge of it were also entrusted with the task of forming an apparatus for illegal work if

---

[1] C. Haldane, *op. cit.*, pp. 182f.   [2] *Ibid.*, p. 266.
[3] P. Toynbee, *Friends Apart* (1954), p. 60.   [4] Hyde, *op. cit.*, pp. 64f.

necessary.[1] The members of this section of the party, who had their own chain of command, would know who the 'cryptos' were and might even include a number of them. As the 'cryptos' could not attend the ordinary party meetings, the similarity between the Communist Party and a democratic, self-governing political organisation, such as it had originally aspired to be, became more and more remote. In fact, its transformation into a military apparatus of the U.S.S.R. was all but complete. Its members were expected, like soldiers, to be willing to sacrifice their lives, if need be, for their ideals – which were regarded as coincidental with the interests of the Soviet Union.

One way in which Communists could work on behalf of the Soviet Union was by espionage. In this activity open members of the party were at a disadvantage, for they were automatically suspect. One party member who engaged in espionage at Woolwich Arsenal – it was Percy Glading, who had been one of the emissaries to India in the nineteen-twenties – was fairly easily caught, with the assistance of an informer, and was sentenced to six years' penal servitude in 1938.[2] But Scotland Yard apparently never got its hands on his contact with the Red Army system, who was a Hungarian Communist with the cover name of 'Stevens' – a man who sounds suspiciously like the 'J. Peters', *alias* 'Stevens' who figured in Whittaker Chambers's evidence in the case of Alger Hiss.[3] Chambers has also recorded the fact that the Red Army, having effectively established a network in the United States, was in the middle nineteen-thirties attempting to extend this American network back across the Atlantic into Britain.[4]

The more direct links with Moscow through the British party were also used for the recruitment of spies, though it is significant that the most successful agent of whom we know was not in fact a member of the party. This was Alexander Foote, who after serving as an ambulance driver in Spain, was recruited to the Soviet network by Springhall, the London District organiser of

[1] Hyde, *op. cit.*, p. 91.
[2] *The Times*, 4 Feb. and 15 Mar. 1938.
[3] W. Chambers, *Witness* (1953), pp. 29f.   [4] *Ibid.*, pp. 252f.

the C.P.G.B.[1] Foote was detailed to work as a wireless operator in an apparatus in Switzerland, and his transmissions were to prove of vital importance for the military conduct of the war by the Soviet leaders. Foote has himself commented on the remarkably cold-blooded attitude that the Russian authorities took to their agents, who were carrying out their work under circumstances of the greatest possible personal risk.[2] It was a general feature of the Soviet attitude: as we shall see, the whole British party, and even the Comintern itself, were regarded as no more than pawns which could readily be sacrificed if the interests of the Russian autocracy demanded the offering of a small gambit.

[1] A. Foote, *Handbook for Spies* (1949), p. 20.   [2] *Ibid.*, p. 157.

CHAPTER VII

IMPERIALIST WAR
AND ANTI-FASCIST WAR, 1939-43

MILITANT though they were, the members of the party were sorely tried by the events of the late summer and autumn of 1939. The twists and turns of Soviet foreign policy were not communicated to them in advance; and the tool of Marxist analysis failed to serve as an adequate substitute. As each major event took place, therefore, the *Daily Worker* would have to give the obvious interpretation in accordance with the current 'line'; but the leading party theoreticians such as Dutt and Emile Burns would at first be inclined to hesitate and to hedge: only after several days' careful thought and consultation of the Soviet press and radio would they endeavour to announce the 'correct' interpretation. Even then, there was a danger of being 'mistaken': and indeed, on the most important question of all – the question of whether to support the British war effort – they discovered that their first interpretation of the situation was completely 'incorrect'. The process of re-orientation was, to say the least, painful.

The immediate reaction of the *Daily Worker* to the announcement of arrangements for a Russo-German non-aggression treaty on 22nd August was to hail it as a 'dramatic peace move to halt aggressors'[1] – a remarkable example of trying to offer two contradictory interpretations at once. This was followed by renewed demands for an Anglo-Soviet pact, coupled with the warning that the Russians had no intention, as Stalin had put it, of 'taking the chestnuts out of the fire' for the Western powers.[2] It was clear, however, that the party leadership still regarded Hitler as a much greater enemy than Chamberlain, who was not 'fascist' but merely 'pro-fascist'. On September 1st, as the invasion of

---

[1] *DW*, 23 Aug. 1939.   [2] *DW*, 26 Aug. 1939.

Poland began, the Central Committee of the party met in London and expressly announced that:

> We are in support of all necessary measures to secure the victory of democracy over Fascism.[1]

The declaration of war followed within forty-eight hours, and at first the party leadership stuck to this forthright attitude. 'The war is here. It is a war that CAN and MUST be won', commented Claud Cockburn, in an unsigned *Daily Worker* editorial on September 4th; and next day the paper's heading ran 'Hitler Touts "Peace" Offer: British and French People Reject Trick'. Harry Pollitt, the general secretary, was meanwhile hastily preparing a pamphlet to elaborate this attitude, which was published about the middle of the month with the title *How to Win the War*. Besides supporting the British war effort, Pollitt even had a good word to say for the Poles:

> The Polish people have had no choice. War has been thrust on them. They have had to fight to defend themselves from a foreign attack whose only purpose is to enslave them to Nazi Germany.[2]

But Pollitt's pamphlet had hardly reached the party bookstalls and the literature secretaries before it became quite obvious that the Soviet Government was pursuing a different 'line'. Its policy was one of benevolent neutrality to Germany, and of co-operation in the dismemberment of Poland, the terms of which had been agreed in a secret annex to the non-aggression pact. On 17th September Russian troops moved into Poland – 'Red Army Takes Bread to Starving Peasants', said the *Daily Worker*[3] – and twelve days later a Soviet-German joint declaration urged the Western powers to accept the new situation and to make peace.

By this time it was clear to some at least of the British Communist leaders that there was an awkward discrepancy between their own official attitude and that of the Russians. It is likely that on the Politburo, which had only five or six members, there was a strong division of opinion as early as 17th September, with Rust and Dutt urging a change in the direction of opposing the war,

---

[1] *DW*, 2 Sept. 1939.   [2] Pollitt, *How to Win the War* (1939), p. 4.
[3] *DW*, 20 Sept. 1939.

and Pollitt and Campbell urging the maintenance of the agreed 'line'. Pollitt, of course, was still the 'leader' of the party, its most important public figure; and Campbell, who was now acting as the editor of the *Daily Worker*, had recovered a certain amount of the influence which he had lost in the *coup d'état* of 1929. On the other hand, Dutt and Rust were the most important members of the party after Pollitt: Dutt was the recognised theoretician of the party, and Rust, since 1929, had been recognised as the ablest and most 'Bolshevik' of the younger leaders. It was under these circumstances of balanced disagreement on the Politburo that power was restored to the Central Committee, which was summoned for the task of adjudicating between the opposing views.

The story of the debate on the Central Committee has never been described in detail. Six months later, however, Dutt gave some account of what happened:

> The debate on the Central Committee on this vital issue lasted over a period of nine days (with interruptions); it was the sharpest and most intense debate in the history of the party; the viewpoint which was finally adopted in the October Manifesto was at first put forward by only a very small minority and became a majority in the course of the debate.[1]

This 'October Manifesto' was published on 4th October; and the 'nine days' of the debate almost certainly included both the preceding weekends, for members of the Central Committee, many of whom were not full-time party workers, had difficulty in meeting in the course of the working week. We may assume, therefore, that it started its deliberations on Saturday, 23rd September. According to Douglas Hyde – not a member of the Central Committee but one who knew many of the members intimately – the Committee had actually agreed on a manifesto in support of the war when it was interrupted by the sudden arrival of Springhall, the British representative at Comintern headquarters, with a message from Moscow.[2] Springhall may have arrived on the 23rd or 24th: certainly not later, and perhaps earlier, for we know that his French colleague, Raymond Guyot, got back to Paris by way of Sweden and England with a similar

[1] *DW*, 8 May, 1940.   [2] Hyde, *I Believed*, p. 70.

message 'about 28th September'.[1] Springhall's message, according to more than one source, was a brief and hasty scrawl from Dimitrov declaring that this was an 'imperialist' war.

The members of the Central Committee, to their credit, did not immediately accept the instructions from Moscow. Pollitt and Campbell continued their opposition and we may well believe that they found strong backing among the more independent members of the Committee such as Arthur Horner and the veteran Tom Mann. Accordingly, the session was adjourned. Meanwhile, events strengthened the hands of those who favoured the Moscow 'line': the French Communist Party accepted it, and then on 26th September was declared illegal by the French Government; even more important, the Soviet-German declaration of 29th September urged the Western powers to make peace. Stalin can hardly have welcomed the prospect of a patched-up peace between Germany and the Western powers; but his act of dissimulation was taken at its face value by the British Communists. Leninist discipline now asserted itself, and the opposition crumbled. Already on the 30th a leader in the *Daily Worker* spoke of 'an entirely new situation' and declared that 'To talk of war to the end, which means the wholesale slaughter of the youth of Europe, would be sheer madness.'

The resolution finally adopted by the Central Committee, which was introduced by Dutt and carried with two dissentients and possibly some abstentions, declared that 'The struggle of the British people against the Chamberlains and Churchills is the best help to the struggle of the German people against Hitler'.[2] Perhaps for the sake of avoiding offence to the more tender susceptibilities on the Committee, it did not say outright that the war was an 'imperialist' one: this conclusion was explicitly drawn only later, in a statement by the Secretariat of the party published in the *Daily Worker* of 12th October. The statement said that the Committee had decided that its earlier views were 'incorrect'; that the British, French and Polish Governments bore 'equal responsibility with German Fascism for the present war'; and that

---

[1] A. Rossi, *Les Communistes Français pendant la Drôle de Guerre* (Paris, 1951), p. 47.   [2] *WNV*, xix, 1015f.

the war was 'unjust and imperialist'.[1] In accordance with these decisions, Pollitt and Campbell, who had so grievously erred, were deprived of their responsibilities at the party centre and were temporarily despatched to work in the provinces, Pollitt in South Wales and Campbell in Scotland. Gallacher took over as general secretary for a time, and Rust resumed the editorship of the *Daily Worker*.

The process by which these decisions were endorsed by the membership provides some indication of the extent to which 'inner party democracy' really existed at this time. According to Dutt, 'The same debate was conducted in every group and organisation of the party with a democratic completeness never before equalled in the history of any party in Britain.'[2] It is true enough that the debate took place, but in effect there was only one side to it: the change of 'line' was a *fait accompli* which its principal opponent, Pollitt, now described as 'correct'[3]; and its endorsement could be regarded as a matter of discipline, a suitable occasion for the assertion of 'centralism' at the expense of 'democracy'. The result was that the District Committees and the membership meetings were as often as not unanimous; here and there a few abstentions took place, and one or two determined and courageous individuals voted in opposition.[4] But the real feeling in the party, which was quite as divided as on the Politburo, got no chance to reveal itself. The only way in which the opponents of the new policy 'voted' was with their feet: they left the party.

*   *   *

There was no doubt of the general unpopularity of Communists with the wider public in the early months of the war. The course of events allowed no respite, for at the end of November Russia invaded Finland, to be met with a fierce resistance which evoked the admiration of the rest of the world, and which was not overcome until March 1940. The Communist attempt to make out that the Russian attack was a 'liberation' of the Finns ('Behind

[1] *DW*, 12 Oct. 1939.   [2] *DW*, 8 May 1940.   [3] *DW*, 13 Oct. 1939.
[4] CP, *Party Organiser*, Nov. 1939, pp. 5f. for the record of membership voting.

the Red Army Life Begins for Finnish People')[1] was too patently absurd to convince anyone who needed convincing. There was also a general feeling that Communist opposition to the war was less worthy than that of the genuine pacifists, who at least had said all along that they were going to oppose it, and who would not have fought for Russia either. Consequently, the party began to suffer from a degree of public hostility that it had not experienced since the early nineteen-twenties. Its propaganda meetings were broken up by angry mobs, and its speakers were assaulted; rescued by the police, they were as often as not taken into custody and charged with using 'insulting words'. Even the distribution of Communist literature was made the excuse for prosecution. Irrespective of the party's policy, it is no wonder that its ranks began to thin out to some extent; and few people can have shared with the eccentric and perverse Claud Cockburn a sense of increased loyalty to the party on the grounds of 'not leaving the regiment when it is under fire'.[2] Cockburn, who had written the leaders for the *Daily Worker* at the outbreak of war, was still writing them, though from a completely different standpoint, after the October Manifesto. So far as he was concerned, it seemed, it did not matter in which direction the 'regiment' directed its own fire.

There were a good many others, however, who may have been as brave as Cockburn, but who were somewhat more scrupulous about the change of 'line'. Certainly, the switch of policy after five years of consistent anti-fascist propaganda was very difficult to accept. Pollitt himself virtually admitted that he had been convinced by his own rhetoric on this subject, and explained that the Spanish War had strongly influenced him to make the 'error' of over-estimating the Fascist danger abroad and obscuring the 'true role of British imperialism'.[3] Veterans of the International Brigade like Tom Wintringham and George Aitken were among those who left the party at this time. Crypto-Communists and 'fellow-travellers' also lapsed in some numbers.

[1] *DW*, 3 Jan. 1940.
[2] See his reminiscence in *New Statesman and Nation*, 7 Apr. 1956.
[3] *DW*, 23 Nov. 1939.

All this did not by any means result in a party collapse. Many
of the gains made in the later nineteen-thirties were effectively
consolidated when the breach with the rest of the labour movement put them to the test. Thus, for example, although a number
of Spanish War veterans took leave of the party, the International
Brigade Association remained under control, and published a
sharp attack on the unoffending Mr Attlee early in the war.[1] So
too, though Victor Gollancz with righteous indignation swung
his Left Book Club – his personal property – away from contact
with Communism, he was obliged to admit that some of the
local groups founded in association with the club remained as
'bastard C.P. locals'.[2] The National Council of Civil Liberties –
a valuable influence on public opinion, if only because of its
honourable name – was also largely if not entirely responsive to
the party 'line', and performed valuable service in the struggles
against wartime restrictions. But perhaps the most striking success
was in the University Labour Federation, the student organisation
affiliated to the Labour Party. With the help of a certain amount
of pacifist feeling, and in the absence of a number of supporters
of the war who had already joined the forces, the Communists
were able to persuade a conference of this organisation to denounce
the 'imperialist' war.[3] This success was followed by the resignation
of Arthur Greenwood from the presidency of the Federation;
his replacement by D. N. Pritt, who was still on the Labour Party
Executive; and then the expulsion of both Pritt individually and
the Federation as a body from membership of the Labour Party.[4]
A further achievement followed early in 1940 when a conference
of the National Union of Students also passed a resolution against
the war.[5]

As the war intensified in the spring and summer of 1940, however, the gap between the popular temper and the Communist
'line' continued to widen. The *Daily Worker* interpretation of the
events leading to the invasion of Scandinavia gave the reader the
impression that the Western powers were primarily to blame:

[1] *DW*, 28 Feb. 1940.   [2] Gollancz in *Left News*, p. 1465 (Apr. 1940).
[3] *WNV*, xx, 50f.   [4] Labour Party *Report*, 1940, pp. 20, 161-8.
[5] *WNV*, xx, 234.

'The Chamberlain Government and the Reynaud Government', declared a statement of the Politburo, 'have deliberately provoked this extension of the war in Northern Europe by their violation of Norwegian neutrality.'[1] As Victor Gollancz pointed out, this sort of attitude suggested a calculated policy of 'revolutionary defeatism' such as Lenin had formulated in the First World War.[2] In the succeeding months, which brought the collapse of France, the threat of invasion across the Channel, and the heavy air raids on London and other cities, the *Daily Worker* seemed to be implementing this policy by encouraging unrest in the forces and among the civilian population, and by advocating stoppages and strikes in industry. The fall of the Chamberlain Government and the entry of the Labour Party into a coalition led by Churchill made no apparent difference. The Communist-controlled International Brigade Association instructed its members, who were of course experienced soldiers, not to take part in the shaping of the Home Guard. As its journal, *Volunteer for Liberty*, put it:

> To discuss at this moment the organisation of the army we want is not merely wasting time, it is helping the ruling class . . .[3]

To their credit, not all the veterans of the Spanish War, not even all the Communists among them, could stomach this attitude. Tom Wintringham and Hugh Slater were prominent among those who helped in the training of those preparing to resist invasion.[4]

The climax of the Communist campaign against the war effort came with the summoning of the so-called 'People's Convention' at the end of 1940. The Convention, supposedly a broad left-wing movement organised in the first instance by non-Communists, was in fact a 'satellite' body of the usual type: its leaders included the inveterate 'fellow-traveller', D. N. Pritt, and its national organiser was Ben Bradley, a party member who had had much

---

[1] *DW*, 10 Apr. 1940. As we now know, this statement was in fact not far from the truth of the matter. See for example W. L. Langer and S. E. Gleason, *Challenge to Isolation* (1952), pp. 409-19.

[2] Gollancz, *Betrayal of the Left* (1941), pp. 108-53.

[3] *Volunteer for Liberty*, July 1940.

[4] According to Gollancz, *Russia and Ourselves* (1941), p. 100, Slater was expelled from the party for writing a booklet entitled *Home Guard for Victory*.

experience in running such organisations. At a time when the country was straining every nerve to resist an imminent invasion, the provisional committee of the Convention produced a six-point programme, no doubt designed to resemble the six points of the nineteenth-century Chartists. Each of these points in itself was highly laudable as a long-term aim, but their immediate impact, if they had been put into effect, would have been disastrous for the war economy. They ran as follows:

1. Defence of the people's living standards.
2. Defence of the people's democratic and trade union rights.
3. Adequate air-raid precautions, deep bomb-proof shelters, re-housing and relief of victims.
4. Friendship with the Soviet Union.
5. A people's government truly representative of the whole people and able to inspire the confidence of the working people of the world.
6. A people's peace that gets rid of the causes of the war.[1]

The People's Convention met in London on 12th January 1941, and was attended by some two thousand 'delegates', supposedly representing over a million workers.[2] Just nine days later the Home Secretary, Herbert Morrison, invoked the Defence Regulations and placed a ban on the publication of the *Daily Worker*.

Anticipating a general proscription of its activities, the party now intensified its preparations for an illegal existence. A few issues of a clandestine *Daily Worker* were distributed in defiance of the government, just to show that the party could do it, and under Rust's direction a secret chain of printing presses was established throughout the country. Douglas Hyde, of the *Daily Worker* staff, was in charge of these arrangements for a time, but he was then made editor of a cyclostyled daily bulletin, *Industrial and General Information*, which was issued as a legal substitute for the *Daily Worker*. The *I.G.I.* staff were all former *Daily Worker* employees, and the bulletin provided the same type of news that

[1] *DW*, 1 Oct. 1940.
[2] *DW*, 13 and 14 Jan. 1941; *The People Speak*, Official Report of the People's Convention (1941).

the paper had previously provided, though in a slightly different form, so as to avoid suppression. Later on, it was decided to launch an illegal paper designed particularly for circulation among members of the forces; but this plan was abandoned when the German invasion of Russia took place in June 1941.[1]

The preparations for underground activity, together with the dislocations caused by wartime conditions, make it difficult to estimate the total membership of the party in this period. In some spheres, as we have seen, Communist influence remained strong; and at the various by-elections for which it entered candidates the party was able to pick up a certain protest vote which made its performance seem quite as creditable as before the war. Some party publications, too, sold unexpectedly well: the *Labour Monthly*, for instance, increased its circulation from 7,500 in August 1939 to 20,000 in December 1940, and this was in spite of an export ban.[2] In the general monotony of publications supporting the war, no doubt the Communist literature had a certain 'curiosity' value deriving from its distinctively different attitude to the principal questions of the day. In spite of this, there seems to be plenty of evidence that the actual membership of the party went down rapidly at first. According to Ted Bramley, the secretary of the London District: 'For a time we lost members heavily. We remained low when we defended Russia in connection with Finland.'[3] He put the London membership of the party at 3,500 in January 1941, which was only about half the last pre-war figure.[4] In the later months of 1940 London had been suffering from bombing more than most parts of the country, but it is reasonable to suppose that the national party membership must have dropped almost as much, perhaps to less than 10,000. According to Bramley, the London membership recovered in the early months of 1941 to a total of 4,500 – still only about two-thirds of the 1939 figures. This recovery, which took place at a time when the *Daily Worker* was banned, was probably due primarily to recruiting in the large engineering factories such as the Napier aircraft works at Acton – a stronghold of the party

[1] Hyde, *I Believed*, pp. 96-104. [2] *Labour Monthly*, xxiii, 2.
[3] *WNV*, xxv, 378. [4] *WNV*, xxi, 743.

from this time onwards, where, as a Communist shop steward boasted and later proved, it was possible to get a strike 'over a cup of tea'.[1]

★   ★   ★

On 21st June 1941 *World News and Views*, the principal organ of the party in the absence of the *Daily Worker*, published a statement by the official Russian news agency denying the 'obviously nonsensical' rumours of German troop concentrations on the Russian border.[2] Next day, the German invasion of Russia began. This at once caused a complete reversal of the Communist 'line' in Britain, but it was a reversal that took place without much of the hesitation and heartsearching that occurred in September 1939. For a time there was still some talk of the need for a 'People's Government' in Britain, but this had disappeared within less than a month. The ease of the change was due as much as anything to Churchill's prompt declaration of support for the Soviet Union, which was followed on 12th July by the signature of the Anglo-Soviet Mutual Aid Pact. Already on 6th July a Communist by-election candidate at Greenock was withdrawn to avoid 'misunderstanding'[3]; and on 8th July Pollitt, who was once again general secretary, sent out a private letter to the party membership in which he declared that 'In supporting the Churchill Government we do it wholeheartedly without any reservations'.[4] He criticised those party members who felt disappointed

> that the Churchill Government had not lined up with Hitler against the Soviet Union in order to prove some theoretical point about the only line of British Imperialism being to effect a switch of the war against the Soviet Union.

No doubt there remained a certain number of these doctrinaires, who after all were only representing what had been the viewpoint of the party as a whole for the previous eighteen months. But the great bulk of the membership rapidly adapted themselves to the new situation, and set about encouraging higher productivity and discouraging strikes, where previously they had been doing

---

[1] Hyde, *op. cit.*, 111.   [2] *WNV*, xxi, 387.   [3] *WNV*, xxi, 444.
[4] Printed in full in Gollancz, *Russia and Ourselves*, pp. 118-26.

the reverse. By October, when a Shop Stewards' conference was held under party auspices, there was hearty applause for the apparently 'blimpish' remark that

> If a man doesn't pull his weight in war production then, whether he is a labourer or an engineer, he should be put in the army.[1]

Indeed, by now the 'blimps' and the Communists were making common cause in the most remarkable way. Retired generals and civic dignitaries of strong Conservative views appeared on platforms for friendship with the U.S.S.R. Portraits of Churchill and Stalin were carried side by side in demonstrations. The Communist Party at once began a campaign for a 'Second Front in the West', in order to relieve the pressure on the Red Army. And meanwhile the Red Army, though still in retreat, fought so unexpectedly well by comparison with what so many publicists in Britain had anticipated, that the popular enthusiasm for all things Russian soared to unprecedented heights. The Russia Today Society and the Society for Cultural Relations with the U.S.S.R., both of them 'satellite' bodies of the party, were besieged by demands for speakers and literature. The party itself was suddenly borne up on the same wave of Russophile sentiment.[2]

The membership of the party had probably been about 12,000 in June 1941 – that is to say, about two-thirds of the latest pre-war figure. In the following four months, however, it recovered all the ground lost in late 1939 and 1940, and by the end of the year the total stood at the record figure of 22,700.[3] This rapid expansion took place almost without effort on the part of the party workers, for no systematic membership drive had been organised. In November it was decided to launch a vigorous recruiting campaign to begin in the New Year, and the target was announced of a further 15,000 members by the end of March.[4] This was one of the very few Communist recruiting campaigns in its entire history which turned out to be far more successful than had initially been planned. In the first three months of 1942

---

[1] *WNV*, xxi, 676.
[2] For a vivid description of this phase, see Hyde, *op. cit.*, pp. 114-30.
[3] *WNV*, xxii, 206.   [4] Springhall in *Labour Monthly*, xxiv, 149.

COMMUNIST HEADQUARTERS, KING STREET, COVENT GARDEN
As rebuilt after war damage

a total of 25,194 recruits was reported – an increase of party membership amounting to 111 per cent.[1] Most of these new members were manual workers in the large war factories, and some of the most spectacular gains were made in the Midlands, where membership almost quadrupled in these three months, and in Lancashire, where it trebled.[2] The total was now 48,000, and still rising. By the end of September 1942 aggregate membership claimed by the districts had risen to 65,000, and although this has to be regarded as a slightly inflated figure, the regular payment of dues to the party centre in the last quarter of the year indicated an average membership of 56,000.[3]

By this time the *Daily Worker* had been allowed to resume publication. In May the annual conference of the Labour Party had carried a resolution in favour of this, though only by a very narrow majority; and in September Herbert Morrison, himself always a staunch opponent of Communism, gave way to the pressure and withdrew the ban. Although Rust was still available to act as editor, the paper was acutely short of staff, for many of its members had been called into the forces; but it was at least financially well off, as the regular contributions for its support had continued to come in during the twenty months of its suppression. When it reappeared, its tone was completely different from that of January 1941: it was now publishing all the encouraging war news, boosting the production drive in the factories, and urging the immediate opening of a 'Second Front'. Over half a million copies of the first issue were ordered: but owing to the newsprint rationing system the total edition was limited to 75,000.[4]

*   *   *

But a further move in the rehabilitation of the Communist Party was still to come. In May 1943 it was reported that the Executive Committee of the Comintern had decided on the dissolution of the International. The Executive's resolution pointed out how

[1] *WNV*, xxii, 206.   [2] *Ibid.*   [3] *Ibid.*, 479; xxiii, 221.
[4] W. Rust, *Story of the Daily Worker* (1949), pp. 97-99.

> The organisational form for uniting the workers chosen by the First Congress of the Communist International . . . has more and more become outgrown by the movement's development and by the increasing complexity of its problems in the separate countries, and has even become a hindrance to the further strengthening of the national working-class parties.[1]

It then referred to the resolution of the Seventh World Congress of 1935, which emphasised the need to avoid interference in the internal affairs of the national sections, and pointed out that it had recently become desirable to disaffiliate the American Communist Party, so as to avoid its being declared illegal under the Voorhis Act of the United States Congress. It therefore proposed that in view of 'the growth and political maturity of the Communist Parties and their leading cadres' the Comintern should be dissolved.

As a matter of form, the constituent parties were consulted before the dissolution took effect. Needless to say, the replies were in full agreement with the proposal. The Central Committee of the C.P.G.B. dutifully echoed the reasons given in the E.C.C.I. resolution:

> As a result of the development of the mass struggle against Fascism, the complicated character of the problems in the separate countries, and the growth of firmly-established Communist Parties . . .[2]

On receipt of the bulk of the replies, the E.C.C.I. determined the formal date of its dissolution as 10th June, 1943, and appointed a small committee consisting of Dimitrov, Manuilsky, Ercoli (*alias* Togliatti) and Pieck to wind up the organisation.[3]

How far was this act of dissolution a genuine act, and how far were the reasons given for the gesture the true motives of the Comintern leaders? Clearly, the Comintern had long ceased to be a real forum of international discussion, where matters could be thrashed out without regard to considerations of national interest. Nor was the Comintern Secretariat any longer exercising the detailed supervision of party activities abroad in the way that it had done in the nineteen-twenties and early nineteen-thirties. As we have seen, these functions had been severely curtailed some

[1] *DW*, 24 May 1943.   [2] *DW*, 25 May 1943.   [3] *DW*, 11 June 1943.

five years before the war – in fact, as soon as the Soviet Government had sought the alliance of the Western powers against the threat of German aggression. Since the drastic surgery of the Stalinist *coup d'état* in each of the major parties, the close adherence of the national sections to the current Soviet 'line' could be assumed, and their leaders could be relied on to listen to Moscow radio if in any doubt about the nature of any changes of policy. The prestige of the Red Army, which was slowly winning its war against the German invasion forces, could be trusted to keep at bay for some time any tendency in other countries towards a theory of 'national Communism'.

Under these circumstances, the maintenance of the formal structure of the Comintern became a matter of no great moment, and Stalin's suspicions of those in any way connected with the Comintern no doubt combined with his low opinion of the parties of Western Europe to lead him to the conclusion that the sacrifice – perhaps only temporary – of this link with the parties abroad was well worth while in the interests of Allied unity. Anything which would tend to increase the Western Powers' willingness to send munitions to Russia and to undertake an early offensive in the rear of the German armies was likely to commend itself to the Russian dictator after almost two years of land warfare against the full weight of the German onslaught. If such was his calculation, Stalin could have derived some satisfaction from the reaction of the London *Times*, which declared that

> The most inveterate British – or, more commonly, American – fears of dark and deep-seated Russian designs to subvert the social order throughout the world will hardly survive the dissolution of the once dreaded, but now long impotent, Communist International.[1]

The British party certainly also stood to gain by the timing of the Comintern announcement. A Labour Party Conference was to take place in June, and for several months the Communists had been renewing their agitation for affiliation. In reply, the National Executive of the Labour Party had been emphasising the significance of the Comintern constitution, with its strongly centralised

[1] *The Times*, 26 May 1943.

formal structure, as a reason for not accepting the party's application: indeed, they went so far as to publish it in full in a circular.[1] But in the upshot the dissolution of the Comintern did not make as much difference to the debate as might have been expected, perhaps because some of the unions with the big block votes had decided to vote against affiliation before the dissolution was announced. Then too an extremely skilful speech was made by Herbert Morrison, who used the full authority of his post as Home Secretary to hint at the unscrupulous character of the Communist leadership. The result was that the Executive's action in rejecting the Communist application was approved by almost three to one.[2]

And so, although it had made gains of considerable importance as a result of the sudden popularity of the Soviet Union, the final seal of respectability was denied to the British Communist Party. It was still not accepted as a 'normal' element in British political life, as an organisation worthy of affiliation to the Labour Party, as the I.L.P. and even the B.S.P. had been accepted in earlier years. At the moment of its greatest expansion of membership and prestige, it still remained outside the pale of national politics – by edict of the trade union officials and the Labour Party Conference. Its leaders tried hard to 'Anglicise' the party in the eyes of the British public, by holding a National Congress in July 1943 – the first for five years – and by deciding to hold annual Congresses in future. They changed the nomenclature of the main elements of its structure to conform to British practice, transforming the Central Committee into the 'Executive Committee', the Politburo into 'Political Committee', factory cells into 'groups' and locals into 'branches'.[3] Indeed, it was remarkable how keen they were to emphasise the distinctively British character of the party just at the time when it had obtained such an accession of membership as a result of its links with the Soviet Union. Yet in truth, little had changed. The Political Committee

[1] *The Labour Party and the Communist Party* (Feb. 1943).
[2] Labour Party *Report*, 1943. pp. 159-68.
[3] The Congress was held in the Hudson's Bay Company's Beaver Hall in London. *DW*, 3 July 1943.

still had the same power as the Politburo before it; the same leaders, with only a very few changes, remained in control of the party as had led it from 1929 onwards, and their real standpoint was as before. Indeed, at the very moment of the dissolution of the Comintern, when the ties which linked the British party to Moscow were supposedly being cut, one of the party's most prominent officers was engaging in incautious acts of military espionage on behalf of the Soviet Union which shortly led to his apprehension.

On 28th July 1943, David Springhall, the national organiser of the Communist Party and a member of its Politburo since his return from Russia in 1939, was convicted on charges under the Official Secrets Act. He was sentenced to seven years' penal servitude for obtaining secret information from an Air Ministry employee, with the intention of passing it to the agents of a foreign power; and it later transpired that he had also been receiving information from an army officer who was engaged in secret work.

When Springhall's conviction was announced, Pollitt at once issued a statement declaring that the party had had no knowledge of the alleged espionage; and Springhall was expelled from the party.[1] This, of course, would be normal procedure, and – as Herbert Morrison pointed out in the Commons – in itself is without value in determining how far Springhall's activities were authorised by his colleagues.[2] As we have seen in the case of Alexander Foote, Springhall had evidently been a party 'contact man' for the Soviet military intelligence for some time. But for such a person to undertake the actual work of passing information to Soviet sources was, as Douglas Hyde says, a 'major indiscretion'[3] both because of the loss of prestige to the party if he was caught, and because of the fact that a prominent Communist would automatically be under the surveillance of the authorities. There are two possible reasons for his action. The information being sought may have been of such exceptional urgency that he was

---

[1] CP, *Report of Executive Committee to 18th Congress* (1944), p. 14.
[2] *Parl. Deb.*, ser. 5, cccxci, 2441f. (5 Aug. 1943).
[3] Hyde, *op. cit.*, p. 144.

induced to throw caution to the winds. Such a situation occurred in Canada shortly afterwards, when the leaders of the Canadian Communist Party were committed to the task of securing the secrets of the atomic bomb. Or it may be that Springhall himself was a man of great zeal who lacked that degree of perspicacity which is necessary for successful intelligence work, and so allowed himself to take unnecessary risks. On the whole, the second interpretation seems more plausible than the first. Springhall had made his way into the inner leadership group of the party more by qualities of toughness and devotion than by any marked intellectual capacity. He was a good man in a stand-up fight, but not much use for the devious methods of espionage.

And so, in order to attempt to preserve the new air of party respectability, Springhall had to be immediately jettisoned by his colleagues. But it is reasonable to suppose that some other party member or sympathiser took on the responsibilities that he had held for contact with the Soviet espionage network. Behind the changing 'face' of the party, the blind loyalty to Moscow which had become established in the previous decades retained its grip upon the leadership.

CHAPTER VIII

THE AFTERMATH:
OPPORTUNITY AND FAILURE

NEARLY sixty thousand members, and permission from Moscow to shape the details of their own policy! Such a situation meant much for the British Communist leaders' feelings of self-esteem, and fed their ambitions for the achievement of real political power. Already they had acquired a degree of respectability and prosperity that would have seemed unattainable only two years earlier. The party was now widely regarded as a sort of special Anglo-Russian Friendship Committee, which even anti-Communists felt they had to treat with scrupulous politeness, at least while Russia was our ally. Many of its new recruits must have joined more as a gesture of solidarity with the Russians fighting at Stalingrad than for any reasons of genuine political conviction. But at least they joined: and in those wartime days of high wages and little to spend them on, the party was able to build up its funds for future activity and for the day when the *Daily Worker* could purchase a printing-press of its own.

And yet, as it turned out, the 1943 membership figures formed a climax which it proved impossible to surpass. Instead of providing a firm basis for further advance as the war progressed, a membership of sixty thousand soon became a smooth and slippery pinnacle of attainment beneath which constant effort was required to prevent speedy retrogression. Already before the end of 1943 it became obvious that the new recruits to the party would be difficult to retain. Many of them, who were primarily interested in winning the war, were taken aback by the extent of the political responsibilities that were now thrust upon them. Not a few were repelled by the arrogant, Calvinistic attitude of the old hands, who demanded herculean labours of the new recruits as a test of acceptance. R. W. Robson, who had served many years as a party organiser, showed alarm at the prospect of losing the new members so unexpectedly gained, and hastened to point out:

> We cannot expect and must not demand of the average new member the same standard of activity as we get from the older comrades. . . . The party has a place within its ranks for every sincere supporter of its policy who is willing to pay his or her dues and participate in some way in the ordinary life of the group or branch.[1]

This was a striking break with the Leninist conception of the Bolshevik elite: but it was a change which sooner or later every Communist party had to make if it was to become a 'mass' party, for the number of persons in any society who are willing to undertake a high degree of political activity is inevitably limited. Robson's views undoubtedly shocked a section of the older membership, but they were supported by the Executive Committee, which went so far as to issue a declaration that:

> There should be no question of striking out any member who pays his dues and supports the policy of the party, on the grounds that he does not yet do more, or has failed to attend meetings. Under the present conditions this is all that should be regarded as the obligatory minimum required of all members.[2]

As a result of this decision great importance began to be attached to the role of the dues-collector, whose job it was to go round the inactive members to collect their subscriptions. This was, of course, very much the situation in many of the branches of the older 'Social-Democratic' parties which Dutt had held up for criticism in his Commission report of 1922.[3] Gone now, at least from the minds of the party leadership, was the old ideal of a Communist Party in which 'every member would have to be a working member'. The first essential now was not quality but quantity of members.

All the same, it was only with the greatest difficulty that the total was held up to something like the level it had reached in the summer of 1943. Early in 1944 it proved difficult to secure the registration of the new recruits for a further year, and by 1st

---

[1] *WNV*, xxiv, 30.   [2] *Ibid.*, p. 95.   [3] See above, p. 21.

March only 38,661 names were listed, compared with over 55,000 at the end of 1943.[1] After making allowances for the upsets of the time – the extension of the military call-up, the movements of troops and civilians and the invasion of Normandy – it still seems clear that political factors must have helped to halt the progress of the party.[2] It is certainly true that the opening of the long-awaited 'Second Front' removed the strongest plank of the party's immediate programme, and led the public to concentrate its attention far more upon the progress of the British and American forces than upon that of the Red Army. The other themes of Communist propaganda at the time seemed rather tawdry by comparison: there was a long and bitter campaign against the release from prison of the now completely discredited Oswald Mosley: and with the assistance of the National Council of Civil Liberties, a sustained fire of criticism was directed against anti-semitism among the Polish forces in Britain. Then in late 1944 and early 1945 the party had much to say about the suppression of the 'partisans' in Greece. But it was now too deeply committed to the support of the Churchill Coalition to adopt a radical standpoint on any major domestic questions. An increase in dues from one shilling to one-and-fourpence a week, which was introduced at the 1944 Party Congress, can hardly have been a major factor in discouraging recruitment.

Meanwhile the leadership was pressing ahead with its policy of 'Anglicising' the party, so as to give it the appearance of a democratic organisation in the tradition of the British labour movement. Early in 1945 a new system of organisation was introduced, which virtually abandoned the attempt to make the factory group the primary unit, and now instead placed emphasis on the 'branch', which co-ordinated members' activities on the basis of their places of residence.[3] In this way the party could most effectively mobilise its members for electoral activity. This was one more step away from the Leninist pattern accepted in 1922. At the same time, the annual Congress and the free vote to elect

[1] *WNV*, xxiv, 86.
[2] For Membership figures later in the year, see *WNV*, xxiv, pp. 122, 399.
[3] *WNV*, xxv, 90.

the Executive were maintained, although at some cost of embarrassment to the leadership. At the 1944 Congress, for instance, the lack of effective discussion inside the party, combined with the great weight given in Congress representation to the 'higher organs' of the party (the District Committees) resulted in the election of an Executive consisting almost entirely of full-time workers at the party centre. Advocates of the 'panels' system were later to seize upon this result as a proof of the disadvantages of attempting to 'democratise' a Communist party.[1] But for the time being the public exercise of democratic forms was regarded as essential for the role which the party was now expected to play.

The new role for the British party, although evidently devised by the party's own leaders rather than by Moscow, was not one which showed any sign of independent thinking, or even any effective assessment of the peculiar characteristics of British politics – rather the reverse. Its basic principle was the maintenance of Russian influence in the post-war world; its starting-point was the Yalta agreement of February 1945; its method was drawn from that of the continental Communists, and especially the French party, which had made such signal gains as a result of participating in a coalition under General De Gaulle. At a meeting of the Executive Committee shortly after the Yalta Conference, Palme Dutt made a long report on the French Communist Party, and the meeting issued a statement which declared:

> We must work to end a position where the Labour Party in Britain is out of step with the Socialist Parties of Europe. We must find the best means through which we can immediately strengthen and broaden national unity so that the Crimea decisions can be carried out with the full backing of the country. No serious-minded people in any section of the Labour and Progressive movement can stand where they did before the Crimea Conference.[2]

What this meant in practice for Britain was indicated the following month in a statement by Pollitt: there should be a 'new National Government' which should include 'representatives of all parties supporting the decisions of the Crimea Con-

[1] CP, *Report of the Commission on Inner Party Democracy* (1957), pp. 18f (Majority Report).   [2] *WNV*, xxv, 61f.

ference'.[1] Believing that Winston Churchill, with all the prestige of an architect of victory, would be invincible at the polls, the party favoured the maintenance of the coalition after the end of the war – or, as Dutt put it, 'the firm united stand of the majority supporters of Crimea in all the principal parties'.[2] It was assumed that this coalition would be re-formed after the General Election, in which, of course, the Communist Party would do sufficiently well to become an important element. In anticipation of electoral agreements to secure this outcome, the party in April reduced the number of its prospective candidates from fifty-two to twenty-two.[3]

Unfortunately for the Communists, the Labour Party leaders were in no mood for a coalition, having decided, with a shrewder sense of political realities, that they stood a good chance of winning an election as an independent force; and having long held the view that any agreement with the Communist Party would be much more of a liability than an asset at the polls. In spite of a sizeable minority vote, they were able to carry this policy at the Easter Conference of the party, which determined their strategy for the election.[4] They rightly assumed that for the British electorate the European victory would be a decisive turning-point, and that the current enthusiasm for a planned economy – based in part on the success of wartime planning in Britain, but also strengthened, rather ironically, by the apparent vindication of Socialist methods in Russia – would redound to the advantage of their own cause.

The German surrender took place in May, and the General Election followed in July. Its result was a severe shock to the Communist Party, which even without any electoral agreement expected to win a number of seats in Parliament. It was especially galling that at a time when the Labour Party swept the country, their own representation was limited to two. Gallacher was re-elected for West Fife, and in the predominantly Jewish constituency of Mile End Phil Piratin succeeded in ousting a Labour M.P. of indifferent quality. Pollitt polled over fifteen thousand votes at

[1] *Ibid.*, p. 89.
[2] *Labour Monthly*, xxvii, 103.
[3] *DW*, 18 Apr. 1945.
[4] Labour Party *Report*, 1945, pp. 81f.

East Rhondda, and was less than a thousand behind the sitting Labour member; but no other Communist was within reach of victory, and the loudly publicised candidatures of Dutt at Sparkbrook (Birmingham) and Rust at South Hackney were both poorly supported by the electors. No less than twelve of the Communist candidates lost their deposits, out of the twenty-one who finally went to the poll. It is true that several 'crypto-Communists' were elected as Labour M.P.s: but this was little consolation for a party which thought it had acquired a respectability of its own; and in the existing situation the 'cryptos' could not reveal their true colours without bringing further discredit on the party.

At the local elections in the autumn of 1945 and the spring of 1946, the Communists did a little better, probably owing to the apathy of the electorate in general. The number of Communist councillors throughout the country rose to 206, the principal strength being in Wales and Scotland.[1] Mile End again provided the party's most striking success in England: here, two Communists, Jack Gaster and Ted Bramley, were elected to the L.C.C. But there were no local authorities under Communist control, and the party had secured little to compensate for the absence of an effective group at Westminster.

Not unnaturally, the discontent of the membership at these political miscalculations and failures sought expression at the 1945 Party Congress. The greater publicity permitted by the 1943 party constitution enables the observer to perceive some indications of this discontent, but these indications only serve to emphasise the fundamentally undemocratic character of the party structure. Among the resolutions down for debate was the following revealing statement from the Acton branch:

> This Congress is of the opinion that our party during years of war has made more wrong assessments and consequent mistakes in policy than is compatible with our claim to be a scientific leadership of the labour movement.
>
> We attribute these mistakes largely to a tendency within our party for the rank and file membership automatically to accept the direc-

[1] *WNV*, xxvi, 129.

tives given from a leadership which, however capable, is nevertheless not infallible.[1]

The Acton branch went on to urge that the full-time organisers of the party should return to their 'normal occupations' for at least twelve months after every two years of office, so as to re-fresh their contacts with the workers and to allow new leaders to develop. This course, it need hardly be said, was not adopted by the Congress; and the Executive, which was again elected without a recommended list, again consisted almost entirely of full-time party workers in London – so much so, indeed, that not long afterwards it felt obliged to co-opt half a dozen industrial workers from the provinces in order to strengthen its national influence.[2]

Although there was a conflict between those who were in favour of more democracy in the party and those who wanted to return to the panel system, hardly anyone was satisfied with the existing method of electing the Executive, and the Congress therefore decided to appoint a Party Commission to enquire into the working of what it called, in the Russian fashion, 'inner party democracy'. The members appointed to the Commission were predominantly full-time party workers, and Dutt was its chairman: so it was natural that its main proposal for reform should be of a conservative character – namely, that the party should return to the principle of the recommended list, though this time with a ballot instead of an open vote. It was maintained that only the recommended list system could ensure that the membership of the Executive would be drawn from a wide variety of talent and experience within the party, with due recognition for different areas and occupations. This proposal was adopted by the Executive in May 1946, accepted by the branches, and put into effect at the 1947 Congress.[3] But the real problem of 'inner party democracy' remained unsolved: it lay in the absence of effective discussion in the party press and at its meetings,

[1] CP, *18th Congress Resolutions and Agenda* (1945), p. 70.
[2] *WNV*, xxvi, 29.
[3] *Ibid.*, p. 162; CP, *Report of Executive Committee to 19th Congress* (1947), p. 20.

and in the absence of free election in the District Committees, quite as much as in the difficulty of securing a representative national Executive.

It is certainly hard to see how the party could have developed a fuller and more open system of control, without losing all contact with the Leninist principles to which it was still supposed to be committed. The contradictions between theory and practice in this event would have become embarrassingly acute. It was difficult enough already to endeavour to construct a 'mass' party out of a sectarian group, for there were always those who would point out that the Communists were not supposed to be more than the 'vanguard' of the working class. For the 'mass', there was the Labour Party; and the logical conclusion of this argument was that the Communists had a responsibility to win recruits for the Labour Party as well as for their own organisation. The point was put to the 1945 Congress by the Bournemouth Borough Aggregate, which argued that 'The only mass political party of the British working class is, and should be, the Labour Party'.[1] There was some truth in Pollitt's reply: 'The fundamental reason why our party does not grow is that you comrades do not want it to grow.'[2]

But whatever the discontent about the misjudgments of the war years, there were no serious problems of future policy to divide the party and to bring out into public view its internal inconsistencies and fundamental lack of democratic control. The leaders were criticised for failing to foresee the Labour victory at the polls, but since the General Election was over, there was nothing that could be done about this. There were some sharp words about the failure of the Executive to detect and denounce the 'errors' of Earl Browder in the United States, which had resulted in the transformation of the American party into a 'political association' until he was overridden by the superior authority of the French Communist leader Jacques Duclos.[3] But

---

[1] CP, 18th Congress Resolutions and Agenda (1945), p. 68.

[2] CP, Report of 18th Congress (1945), p. 35.

[3] WNV, xxv, 370. For the strictures of Duclos on 'Browderism' see Labour Monthly, xxvii, 239.

this was not a matter which could really be regarded as of any fundamental importance for the British party, even if it did indicate the apparent theoretical weaknesses of the leadership. The existing party 'line' of critical support for the Labour Government was, in 1945 at least, virtually unassailable.

*   *   *

In the midst of all its frustrations there was one sphere in which the party made rapid and important progress in these years. This was its trade union activity. It was typical of the British party that these successes took place as much by accident as by design. Like the nineteenth-century rebel Bakunin, who, according to Mr Alan Taylor, was present in a revolutionary situation at Dresden only because he had missed his train,[1] the British Communists had a knack of being caught facing in the wrong direction when the signal of opportunity was given. The enthusiastic efforts of the Communists in the factories from 1941 onwards, which were primarily for the sake of helping the Russians, won them the respect of their fellow-workers, and already by 1943 the T.U.C. General Council had been more or less forced to withdraw the 'Black Circular' of 1934 which prevented trades councils from accepting Communists as delegates.[2] Although the Communist Party was now primarily interested in building up for itself a strong electoral position, some of its full-time organisers were conscripted for work in the factories, and were thus obliged to devote themselves to building the industrial strength of the party.[3] At the beginning of 1945 Kerrigan noted the fact that the membership strength was 'overwhelmingly weighted in favour of engineers and aircraft workers'[4]; but factory organisation of the party was now virtually abandoned, and all efforts were concentrated on the building of the residential branches and their

[1] A. J. P. Taylor, *From Napoleon to Stalin* (1950), p. 59.
[2] T.U.C. *Report*, 1943, pp. 337-9.
[3] For example, Finlay Hart, a party organiser, was directed by the Ministry of Labour to work in a Clyde shipyard. He became a shop steward. See the brief biography in *WNV*, xxxi, 146f.
[4] *WNV*, xxv, 23.

electoral activity, the failure of which we have already recounted.[1]

At the same time, the Communists were committed to a policy of working with and through the existing trade union structure, and it is hardly surprising that they began to have their successes in this field. To some extent it was simply a matter of consolidating old strongholds: the Welsh and Scottish miners' unions, for instance, and the Foundry Workers, who in 1944 elected Jim Gardner, a foundation member of the party, as their national secretary. In another case, that of the Fire Brigades Union, the success seemed to be almost accidental, following as it did the election of John Horner, who was not known to be a party member, as general secretary in 1939.[2] Bob Darke, a member of the union during the war, has described how he himself, as a Communist, was suddenly spirited onto the Executive Committee and how the union took up the party's agitation for a 'Second Front' to help the Russians.[3] But the most striking feature of the growth of the party's strength in the unions was its rapid progress in the London organisations of the big factory unions – the Amalgamated Engineering Union, the Transport and General Workers Union, and the Electrical Trades Union. The national organisation of the Electrical Trades Union, which was much more of a Londoners' union than the others, fell under the control of the party, with a Communist President and assistant secretary[4]; and the London Trades Council, after the election of Julius Jacobs as secretary in 1945, followed the same course.[5] In the Transport and General Workers Union – the largest union in the world – Bert Papworth, the Communist busmen's leader, was in 1944 chosen as one of its two representatives on the T.U.C. General Council.[6]

[1] CP, *Report of Executive Committee to 18th Congress* (1945), pp. 9f.; *Report of 18th Congress*, pp. 79f.

[2] F. H. Radford, *Fetch the Engine* (1951), p. 109.

[3] 'Bob' (C.H.) Darke, *Communist Technique in Britain* (1952), pp. 72-5.

[4] F. Foulkes and W. C. Stevens respectively. The latter became secretary in 1947.

[5] Jacobs had been defeated by one vote in 1937. See (G. K. Tate), *London Trades Council History, 1860-1950* (1950), p. 152.

[6] V. L. Allen, *Trade Union Leadership* (1957), p. 272.

EXECUTIVE COMMITTEE IN SESSION, JANUARY 1948

Among those present may be seen Peter Kerrigan (front row, left); John Gollan (front row, centre); William Rust (second row, second from left)

If it took the party some time to realise the importance of the successes it was achieving in the unions, it took the Labour Party even longer. So long as Communist policy was not violently at odds with that of the Labour Party, the rank and file of the unions concerned were not likely to be worried about having Communist officers, and might not even be aware of the fact. In some unions, notably the A.E.U., the complicated structure of control undoubtedly assisted a determined minority like the Communists; and in all of them the apathy of the membership at large acted as a valuable ally of the party.[1] In some cases too there is reason to believe that members of the party concealed their political loyalties in order to allay the suspicions of non-Communist members.

The success of Communist penetration of the unions in these years was especially remarkable by contrast with their abject failure at the polls. It is no exaggeration to say that they were very nearly in control of the trade-union movement: for their strength in the leadership of the mining and engineering unions had almost reached a decisive point, and in the Transport and General Workers Union the party by 1946 had nine open members in a General Executive Council of thirty-four, and three members out of eight on the more powerful Finance and General Purposes Committee.[2] This success in Ernest Bevin's own union was to a large extent the fruit of the pre-war policy of consolidating the union with a view to its eventual permeation, at the expense of possible early success in the control of a small 'break-away' such as the attempted busmen's union of 1937. Bob Darke, himself a bus conductor and a member of the party's Industrial Policy Committee, which was responsible for co-ordinating all these efforts at control, has recorded how much importance was attached to winning the T.G.W.U. with its million and a quarter votes available for use at the T.U.C. and at Labour Party conferences.[3]

[1] For a study of the relationship between Communist infiltration and rank-and-file apathy in London branches of the T. & G.W.U., see J. Goldstein, *Government of British Trade Unions* (1952). See also, more generally, B. C. Roberts, *Trade Union Government and Administration in Great Britain* (1956), pp. 248-59.

[2] Allen, *op. cit.*, p. 273.   [3] Darke, *Communist Technique in Britain*, p. 65.

K

Unfortunately for the party, the course of international affairs set its plans awry. The beginnings of the 'cold war' and the initiation of the Marshall Plan in 1947 placed the Communists in direct opposition to the policy of the Labour Government, and the extent of Communist infiltration into the union control was then generally recognised and vigorously combated.

*   *   *

Meanwhile the national membership of the party had begun to fall with alarming speed. At first this was clearly due to disappointment with the results of the General Election, and a feeling that the new Labour Government deserved a chance to justify its election programme. The determination with which the government put through its legislative programme prevented any considerable disillusionment among its supporters on the Left; and the creation of the National Health Service and the enactment of other measures designed to extend the sphere of social security could not but offer some substance to the view that economic change could be effected by constitutional means. At the same time, the man in the street was inclined to blame the Russian rather than the British Government for the deterioration of relations between the two countries. British soldiers returning from occupation zones in Europe brought back unfavourable reports of the behaviour of Russian troops and their commanders; and the growing unpopularity of the Soviet Union inevitably had its effects on the membership figures of the party. The Canadian spy trial and the case of Allan Nunn May served as reminders of the close links between the party and the Soviet Union, although in neither case was any of the senior officials of the British party implicated.[1]

Thus it was that in spite of renewed recruiting campaigns Communism lost ground in Britain in the immediate post-war years. At the end of April 1946 the total membership had sunk to 42,123, and branches were being urged to 'establish the regular practice of card inspection at all meetings of party members'.[2]

[1] See *Report of the Royal Commission* (Ottawa, 1946), p. 513, for one minor C.P.G.B. member who figured in the case.   [2] *WNV*, xxvi, 198.

A new drive for recruits in the spring of the year brought in only 2,000 members in three months, which was hardly enough to make up the constant wastage[1]; and in June of the following year the total had fallen still further to 38,579.[2] A serious portent for the future was the decline of support among the young. The Y.C.L. shrank to less than 1,500 members, and was thus only about one-third of its pre-war size, although the pre-war party as a whole was less than half the size of the post-war party.[3] As for the intellectuals, there were plenty of them still in the party: to mobilise their talents, a 'National Cultural Committee' was formed in 1947, and the Historians' Group alone had over a hundred members.[4] But among undergraduates the former virtual monopoly of left-wing organisation achieved by the Communist-controlled Student Labour Federation (formerly University Labour Federation) was now challenged by groups supporting the Labour Party, which formed a National Association of Labour Student Organisations in 1947.

Under these circumstances the high hopes of a mass circulation for the *Daily Worker* began to seem unreal, in spite of the financial resources which the paper had built up during the war. In 1945 the circulation was just about 100,000 copies a day,[5] and the immediate programme envisaged by William Rust, its energetic editor, was to increase this to half a million, using a new rotary press which was already on order.[6] Further large sums for the development of the paper were raised by launching a co-operative ownership scheme, under the name of the 'People's Press Printing Society'[7]; and a site for the press was bought in Farringdon Road, on which it was eventually decided to erect an entirely new building. With Rust in control and such able newspaper men as Allen Hutt, Walter Holmes and 'Frank Pitcairn' (Claud Cockburn) on its staff, the paper was not lacking in journalistic quality; and J. B. S. Haldane was still continuing his popular weekly articles

[1] *WNV*, p. 222. [2] *Ibid.*, xxviii, 99. [3] *Ibid.*, p. 291.
[4] *Ibid.*, xxvii, 395; xxix, 536. [5] *Ibid.*, xxv, 95, 230.
[6] Rust, *Story of the Daily Worker*, pp. 114f.
[7] For details of the P.P.P.S. see 'Report of the Royal Commission on the Press, 1947-9', *Parliamentary Papers*, 1948-9, xx, 23f., and 'Minutes of Evidence' *Parliamentary Papers*, 1947-8, xiv, 935-51.

on scientific subjects. But somehow the news of progress in the
Soviet sphere, now extended to include the whole of Eastern
Europe – the photographs of Communist athletes and the statistics of booming industrial production – all failed to create the
interest that they had had in the nineteen-thirties. After 1945, the
concept of 'planning' lost its romantic attraction for nearly all
sections of the British public. The *Daily Worker*, like the party as
a whole, was faced with a falling market for its wares. The difficulties of the paper could no longer be charged to the wholesalers'
ban, for this had been removed in 1942.[1] The circulation averaged
only about 118,000 in June 1947 – a figure which owing to fresh
newsprint restrictions remained the maximum possible for the
remainder of 1947 and 1948.[2]

There was always an element inside the party which sought a
vigorous anti-Labour policy, even on the very aftermath of the
1945 General Election. At first, while the leadership chose to
support the government, this element could be branded as 'Left-
sectarian' or even 'Trotskyist'. Gradually, however, as relations
between the Western Powers and the Soviet Union became more
strained, the British Communists felt themselves obliged to move
more and more towards the 'Left-sectarian' position in order to
maintain their loyalty to the U.S.S.R. The increasing divergence
between British and Russian foreign policy was at first attributed
to malign influences among the permanent officials of the Foreign
Office; then for a time it was made out to be the personal responsibility of Ernest Bevin; and finally the Labour Government
as a whole was written off as hopelessly reactionary.

It took some time for the final step to be taken, for the party
had followed the policy of critical support for Labour ever since
1941, and as we have seen this had brought most profitable advantages, especially inside the trade-union movement. In February 1947 the Political Resolution of the Party Congress spoke
of 'the reactionary trends in the Labour Government's policy',
and of 'its failure to break through the vested interests that are
holding up improvements in the lives of the working people'.[3]

---

[1] *Parliamentary Papers*, 1947-8, xiv, 935.   [2] *Ibid.*, 1948-9, xx, 18.
[3] CP, 19th *Congress Resolutions and Proceedings* (1947), pp. 12f.

Open opposition, however, was another matter. The change was in large part prompted by the establishment of the Communist Information Bureau, and by the decisions taken at its inaugural conference in Poland.

The Communist Information Bureau, or Cominform as it became known, was in effect a revival of the Comintern, though the Russian control was more blatantly obvious than before, and the British party, among others, was slighted by not being admitted to membership. The member parties, apart from the Russian party, were predominantly those of the Eastern European countries which owed their resurrection and rise to power almost entirely to the victories of the Red Army. The French and Italian parties, the two largest in Europe outside the Soviet sphere, were also represented, and it was probably the former which became responsible for the transmission of any special secret communications for the British party. According to the resolution of the conference, the Information Bureau was to be

> entrusted with the task of organising the exchange of experience, and, if necessary, with the task of co-ordinating the activities of the Communist Parties on the basis of mutual agreement.

The task of 'co-ordinating' was begun at once, with a declaration of policy based on a report by the Russian leader Zhdanov, which involved a switch in the 'line' for all the parties. The world, it declared in what has since become a very hackneyed metaphor, was split into two 'camps';

> Two camps came into being, the imperialist anti-democratic camp with the basic aim of establishing world domination of American imperialism and routing democracy, and the anti-imperialist democratic camp with the basic aim of disrupting imperialism, strengthening democracy, and eliminating the remnants of Fascism.

There was nothing to be said for 'right-wing Socialists' such as Attlee and Bevin, the statement emphasised, for they

> in fact remain in all respects loyal supporters of the imperialists, bringing disintegration into the ranks of the working class and poisoning their outlook.[1]

[1] *WNV*, xxvii, 463f.

In the face of these decisive words there was nothing for the British party to do, if it wished to remain in line with the Russian and European parties, except to copy. Palme Dutt's 'Notes of the Month' in the November issue of the *Labour Monthly* were headed 'Two Camps – One World'[1]; and in December Pollitt delivered a special report to the Executive which declared:

> When the world is clearly divided into an imperialist and an anti-imperialist camp, with a Labour Government as active partner in the imperialist camp, and carrying through a capitalist solution of the crisis, it is necessary that important changes in the policy of the Communist Party to meet this situation should be made.[2]

Among the changes was to be the abandonment of Communist support for increased production. This policy, which had been 'absolutely correct' in the past, would now 'only result in trailing behind the Government's reactionary policy'.[3] With these words Pollitt steered the party firmly into a policy almost as sectarian as that of 'Class Against Class' in 1929-32.

[1] *Labour Monthly*, xxix, 323.   [2] *WNV*, xxvii, 584.   [3] *Ibid.*, p. 585.

CHAPTER IX

THE LAST YEARS OF STALIN, 1948-53

THE initial conference of the Cominform not only provided the Communist parties with a fresh analysis of the international position: it also indicated the policies that they were to pursue, in a concerted campaign against what it conceived to be the aims of the 'imperialist anti-democratic camp'. In the first place, in order to disrupt the operation of the Marshall Plan and Western rearmament, each party was to assume the role of defender of its country's independence against the encroachments of the United States. As the Cominform statement put it:

> They must take into their hands the banner of the defence of the national independence and sovereignty of their own countries.[1]

This meant, for the British party, protests against the American occupation of air bases in Britain and against the acceptance of Marshall Aid. Naturally, such protests coming from a party which had paid so little attention in the past to the maintenance of British sovereignty were bound to appear somewhat artificial. It was a curiously incongruous band of a dozen M.P.s who found themselves in the lobbies together in opposition to the Marshall Plan: half of them were Beaverbrook Imperialists and the other half Communists or fellow-travellers.[2] There were also some strange features of the anti-American campaign into which the party now launched itself, although here it was not difficult to take advantage of latent prejudice now revived by the difficulties arising from the presence of the American forces. Derek Kartun, the Foreign Editor of the *Daily Worker*, who was one of the last British Communists to be allowed to pay a visit to the United States, wrote a series of articles and pamphlets denouncing the 'cheap, hysterical wilderness of American life' where, according

[1] *WNV*, xxvii, 46.4.   [2] *Parl. Deb.* ser. 5, ccccliii, 342 (6 July 1948).

to statistics, 'one serious crime was committed every 18.7 seconds.'[1] The climax of the party's campaign came in 1951 with the mobilisation of its intellectuals for a conference on 'The American Threat to British Culture', at which all the accumulated eighteenth- and nineteenth-century criticisms of the United States, based on aristocratic and anti-colonial snobbery, were pressed into the service of international Communism.[2] All this was in accordance with the Cominform instructions, which, as translated into British circumstances by George Matthews, the party's assistant general secretary, ran as follows:

> Relate every question affecting masses to the issue of national independence. Troops to Korea – it is MacArthur's orders. Two years' military service – it is an American demand. Rearmament – it is American orders. Attack on standards – it is U.S. which insists.[3]

The Cominform conference also instructed the parties to take the lead in a movement for peace and friendship with the Soviet bloc. 'There is a vast gap', said the resolution,

> between the desire of the imperialists to unleash a new war and the possibility of organising such a war. The people of the world do not want war. The forces championing peace are so considerable and large that if these forces remain staunch and firm in the cause of defending peace, if they display endurance and firmness, the aggressors' plans will suffer a complete fiasco.[4]

This declaration at once involved the British party in the elaboration of its structure of 'satellite' organisations to a degree unexampled before the war. Innumerable international 'peace' and 'friendship' societies were created, for each of which there had to be a British affiliate.[5] There were already three societies for friendship with the Soviet Union itself, namely, the Society for Cultural Relations (founded in 1924), the British-Soviet Friendship Society

---

[1] D. Kartun, *America—Go Home!* (1951), p. 5. See also his *This Is America* (1947) and *U.S.A.'53: The Truth Behind Eisenhower* (1953).

[2] *DW*, 30 Apr. 1951; 'The U.S.A. Threat to British Culture', *Arena*, June-July 1951.

[3] *Communist Review*, v (1950), 319.   [4] *WNV*, xxvii, 464.

[5] For a detailed account of these, see Industrial Research and Information Services, *Communist Solar System* (1957).

(founded in 1927 as the Friends of Soviet Russia) and the Scotland-U.S.S.R. Friendship Society (founded in 1945). For the other Eastern European countries under Communist control, the position was more patchy: there was a British-Czechoslovak Friendship League, which was founded during the war and which had come under Communist control: indeed its secretary, a Czech, was in July 1948 expelled from Britain for acting as a link in an espionage system.[1] There was also a British-Yugoslav Association, founded during the war, and a British-Polish Society dating from 1946: both were under party control. To supplement these, a British-Rumanian Friendship Association and a Committee (later Society) for Friendship with Bulgaria were founded in 1948, and, for the sake of the new Communist states in the Far East, a British-China Friendship Association came into existence at the end of 1949 and a British-Vietnam Committee in 1952. As all these bodies were supposed to appear to be independent of the party, it was considered desirable that the chairman should be a prominent fellow-traveller or 'crypto-Communist' rather than an open member of the party. Unfortunately, suitable persons of this type were becoming rare, and those who were available had to do duty for several societies. Thus D. N. Pritt served as President of the S.C.R., as both President and chairman of the British-Rumanian Association, and as President of the Society for Friendship with Bulgaria, apart from all his functions in other types of 'satellite' work; and Commander Edgar Young, who was vice-chairman of the British-Rumanian Society, was also chairman of the Committee for Friendship with Bulgaria and the British Vietnam Committee.

To propagate the idea of 'peace', however, the 'friendship' societies were not enough. There had to be a general organisation to co-ordinate 'peace' propaganda in Britain, affiliated of course to the Cominform's international organisation for the same purpose. The latter, originally the 'International Liaison Committee for Intellectuals for Peace', which was formed after a Congress at Wroclaw in August 1948, became in 1949 the 'World Peace

[1] *The Times*, 22 July 1948.

Council'. A 'British Cultural Committee for Peace' was similarly formed in 1948, and duly became the 'British Peace Committee' in the following year. Although this body secured some support from the more naïve of the genuine pacifists and internationalists, the majority were not taken in: as the General Secretary of the Fellowship of Reconciliation put it,

> It is impossible to ignore the inspiration and influence of the Communist element in the British Peace Committee; and that the methods advocated, or at least not repudiated, by that Communist element, are not consistent with the establishment of a world order based on love.[1]

Such criticism did not deter those running the organisation from building up a complex structure of local and regional committees and also a series of associated bodies catering for each of the professions – a final achievement which was not accomplished until 1951-2 (Authors' World Peace Appeal, Medical Association for the Prevention of War, Musicians' Organisation for Peace, Teachers for Peace, Artists for Peace). For purposes of liaison with other Communist-run world organisations there were also the British Youth Festival Committee (founded 1951) and the National Assembly of Women (1952). The British affiliate of the International Association of Democratic Lawyers was the Haldane Society, originally founded in 1929 as a group of left-wing lawyers, but in due course largely taken over by sympathisers with Communism.[2]

All these bodies, and several more – of which the most important were the well-established 'satellites' like the Labour Research Department and the Student Labour Federation – were at once 'proscribed' by the Labour Party. This meant that their members were technically ineligible for membership of the Labour Party. As new bodies of the same type were created, or as old ones fell under Communist control, the Labour Party's list was extended. This policy usually prevented the 'satellite' bodies

---

[1] *The Times*, 1 July 1950.
[2] In 1949 the Labour Party members of this body seceded to form a Society of Labour Lawyers. *The Times*, 6 Apr. and 19 May 1949.

from attaining any importance, and so to a large extent thwarted
the objects of the Communist Party. It was a policy which also
had its drawbacks, however, for the bodies concerned often had,
to all appearance, a most laudable purpose to serve, and rank-and-
file members of the Labour Party, especially if politically in-
experienced, frequently did not understand the reasons for the
proscription and so harboured feelings of resentment against
'dictatorship' from Transport House. It occasionally happened,
too, that the Communists lost control of a 'satellite' body, owing
to some personal disagreement among the officials, or as a result
of some unforeseen turn of events in the wider political sphere.
At such moments the presence among the membership of a substantial band of loyal Labour Party supporters could have had
devastating effects for the Communist leadership. On balance,
however, the policy of proscription may be regarded as probably
the safest way of dealing with the problem of the 'satellite' bodies,
from the standpoint of the Labour Party officials; and in any case
after some thirty years of operation it has now become a traditional method of defence against Communist infiltration tactics.

The running of all these bodies – the full list of which has by
no means been exhausted – took up much of the time of party
members in this period. It may well be questioned if the effort
was really worth while in the extent to which it provided the
party with effective organs of propaganda to wider circles of the
population (the 'bridge to the masses' which the Communists
always sought). In so far as the Labour Party policy of proscription was successful, the advantage to the British party was certainly kept within bounds. But it must be remembered that a
major purpose of the 'satellite' organisations was to fit into the
international propaganda pattern. The existence of the British
organisations, and their various activities, including, for instance,
the sending of delegations to pay official visits behind the 'Iron
Curtain', served the domestic and foreign propaganda require-
ments of the various Communist governments themselves. Not
having a very large membership in relation to the Communist
parties of other European countries, the British party no doubt
found the whole international paraphernalia much more difficult

to maintain than did, for example, the French party; but the British party had to do its duty to the full, and it could not fail the international agencies by neglecting to form its appropriate committees. Willi Münzenberg, who founded the first 'satellite' propaganda bodies in the early nineteen-twenties, would no doubt have been pleased to see how his system had developed in the succeeding generation, if he had not himself fallen as one of Stalin's victims in 1940.[1]

*   *   *

An acid test of what Communists meant by 'peace' and 'friendship' was provided unexpectedly early in the course of the campaign. Since the end of the war, Yugoslavia had been regarded as the model of the 'People's Democracies' of Eastern Europe. Many in Britain outside the ranks of the party had been thrilled by the wartime exploits of Marshal Tito's 'partisans'; many Communists and non-Communists had enjoyed a visit to Yugoslavia to work on the celebrated 'Youth Railway'; and the portrait of the Yugoslav leader had a prominence on British Communist mantelpieces second only to that of Stalin himself. Leaders of the British party paid visits to Belgrade and returned with glowing accounts of the new country's development: as late as September 1947, for instance, Rust could find in Yugoslavia 'a real democracy where the people rule and build a new life'. In his view at that time Yugoslavia was

> showing to the whole world the miracles that a free people can accomplish when power is in their own hands.[2]

Similarly James Klugmann, another party official, writing at about the same time on the Yugoslav constitution, emphasised the 'deep popular character' of the new state, and described Tito and his colleagues as 'theoreticians of Marxism who know how to use Marxism as a guide for action'.[3]

---

[1] The evidence about his death is not quite conclusive, but he was already out of favour with Stalin. See Ruth Fischer, *Stalin and German Communism* (1948), p. 614n.; A. Koestler, *Invisible Writing* (1954), p. 407.

[2] *DW*, 13 and 15 Sept. 1947.

[3] J. Klugmann, 'Notes on the State and Constitution of the New Yugoslavia', *Modern Quarterly*, iii, 70.

This pattern of enthusiastic approval was rudely disturbed, however, in June 1948, when the Cominform leaders, meeting this time without Yugoslav representatives, denounced Tito as a traitor to Socialism. The Yugoslav Government was charged with various crimes, including those of 'pursuing an unfriendly policy towards the Soviet Union', of 'breaking with the Marxist theory of classes', and of reducing the Yugoslav Communist Party to 'a position of semi-legality'.[1]

The details of the dispute between the Yugoslavs and the Cominform do not concern us here: clearly the trouble had arisen because this was the first instance of a Communist state asserting its independence of the Soviet Union and rejecting the position of subordination into which the other Eastern European states had fallen. On this issue, however, the British party was completely incapable of taking a 'line' of its own, still less of determining that 'line' by an effective attempt at internal discussion. The Political Committee of the party, at its usual Thursday morning meeting on 1st July, decided to present its 'unanimous approval' of the Cominform resolution as a *fait accompli* to the party.[2] Rust at once weighed into the attack on the Yugoslav leaders in an article for Friday's *Daily Worker*,[3] and Pollitt made arrangements to address hastily-summoned 'aggregate meetings' of the party in Glasgow and London. At these meetings there was some opposition to face, in view of the lack of consultation on the matter; but Pollitt used all his fine rhetorical gifts to secure an emphatic vote of confidence for the Cominform 'line'. At the London meeting on 7th July, he admitted that he still knew very little of the substance of the charges against Tito, but he played heavily on the fact that so many well-known Communist leaders had joined in the indictment:

Men like Rakosi, never out of prison for fifteen years; men like Slansky, who was tortured at Dachau, are not men who 'turn when Joe says turn'. Their record in the Communist movement is of such a character as to prove, to me at any rate, that when their signatures

[1] *For a Lasting Peace, for a People's Democracy!* (Bucharest), 1 July 1948. This was the English edition of the Cominform journal, originally published in Belgrade.   [2] *WNV*, xxviii, 288.   [3] *DW*, 2 July 1948.

go on a document it indicates belief and consciousness that what they sign . . . is correct.[1]

Pollitt did not speak in vain, either at Glasgow or in London: at both meetings he obtained endorsement by an overwhelming majority, which in London amounted to 1,000 votes to 2, with 20 abstentions. After this it was easy enough to get the nominal approval of other aggregate meetings elsewhere and also, incidentally, of the Executive Committee – theoretically the supreme authority in the party between Congresses – which did not meet until 9th and 10th July.[2] The only serious difficulty for the British party came in the 'satellite' body called the British-Yugoslav Association. This body contained not only loyal Communists but also a considerable number of individuals who had joined it to express their genuine admiration of the new Yugoslavia. The latter resisted the acceptance of the Cominform 'line' and were sufficiently successful to impose upon the Association the temporary adoption of an attitude of 'neutrality'.

In the course of the following year, 1949, a whole series of Communist leaders in countries bordering on Yugoslavia were arraigned and tried – falsely, as has now been admitted in almost all cases – on charges of collusion with Tito and his colleagues in counter-revolutionary plans for the benefit of 'Anglo-American capitalism'. The principal defendants were Kochi Xoxe in Albania, Rajk in Hungary and Kostov in Bulgaria. In the course of the hearings, a fantastic picture was built up of a cunning British intelligence plot, from 1942 onwards, to use the Yugoslav Communist Party for the purposes of 'imperialist policy'. By the end of the year the Cominform had created such an atmosphere of tension in Eastern Europe that it could begin to incite revolt inside Yugoslavia, declaring that 'The struggle against the Tito clique of hired spies and assassins' was an 'international duty'.[3] Under these circumstances the Communist members of the British-Yugoslav Association felt obliged to break their links with the 'Titoites' in their midst. At a meeting of the Association in November 1949 – over fourteen months after the original Cominform denunciation of Yugoslavia – a resolution to adopt

---

[1] WNV, xxviii, 295.   •   [2] Ibid., p. 294.   [3] DW, 30 Nov. 1949.

the Cominform attitude of hostility to the Tito government was accepted by 72 votes to 57, and the minority of 'Titoites', including a number of well-known 'left-wingers', seceded in order to form a society of their own. D. N. Pritt was elected as the new chairman of the existing Association.[1]

It might have been supposed that the British party would have gone no further than this: many of its members must have hesitated at some of the improbabilities of the supposed 'Anglo-American imperialist' plot – especially, perhaps at the attribution of such outstanding skill to the British intelligence service. But where the Cominform had pointed the way, the foreign editor of the *Daily Worker* was obliged to follow. Derek Kartun, who now occupied this exacting position, attended the Rajk trial in Hungary, reported it for the paper, and published a little book about it entitled *Tito's Plot Against Europe*, which showed that he at any rate was prepared to swallow the whole indictment – perhaps because in his own words it was 'so very much stranger than fiction'.[2] And a little later James Klugmann, carefully putting together all the denigrations of the Yugoslavs that he could lay his hands on, published a substantial volume called *From Trotsky to Tito*, almost every sentence of which was in flat contradiction of his 1947 article on the Yugoslav constitution. 'The lot of the workers in Tito Yugoslavia', he wrote,

> has become a very hard one. Their living conditions have grown steadily worse in the last three years.[3]

Some farms, at least, had been collectivised; but

> Nothing illustrates better the duplicity of Titoism . . . than the phoney collective farms of Tito Yugoslavia.[4]

As for the working of the constitution, which he had previously so lavishly praised,

> Like the people of any colonial or semi-colonial country, the Yugoslav working population faces not only economic but political oppression.[5]

---

[1] *Daily Telegraph*, 18 Nov. 1949.
[2] D. Kartun, *Tito's Plot Against Europe* (1949), p. 7.
[3] J. Klugmann, *From Trotsky to Tito* (1951), p. 126.
[4] *Ibid.*, p. 131.   [5] *Ibid.*, p. 141.

Tito and his colleagues, in short, were hardly different from fascists: they had 'learned their tactics from Hitler and Goebbels'.[1] Only in the other countries remaining in the Soviet sphere were things as they should be:

> In all these countries, there has been a consistent rise of real wages, a consistent development of social services of every description, a consistent increase in the number of men and women employed in industry.[2]

In this way the British party leaders and officials demonstrated their support of the Cominform: but events were to overtake them once more. In 1955 the Russian leaders apologised for the whole campaign against the Yugoslav party, and re-established relations with Tito. In 1956, reluctantly and belatedly, Pollitt was obliged to do the same, on behalf of himself and the lesser functionaries of the British party:

> We, in the Executive Committee of the British Communist Party, were misled by evidence that is now stated to have been fabricated, and we now withdraw our previous attacks on Tito and Yugoslavia – including the statement made by myself at the London membership meeting in 1948 and James Klugmann's book *From Trotsky to Tito*.[3]

*   *   *

Much of the venom of Communist attacks on Yugoslavia arose, of course, from the belief that in a world of 'two camps' any assertion of independence in the 'anti-imperialist camp' was an act of treason. But the intensification of the 'cold war', for which the Russians in the last years of the Stalin dictatorship were so largely responsible, also made things in general increasingly difficult for the Communist parties of Western Europe. Communist strength in the trade unions had to be mobilised for the unpopular purpose of attacking and discrediting the Marshall Plan, and for hindering and even sabotaging rearmament. Such policies rapidly led to the disruption of the World Federation of Trade Unions, in which the Communists had almost a predominent influence; and also, in Britain at least, to a sudden realisation

[1] Klugmann, *op. cit.*, p. 157.   [2] *Ibid.*, p. 188.   [3] *WN*, iii, 248.

of the danger of Communist penetration inside each individual union.

There was no doubt that the degree of Communist control in the British trade union movement was out of all proportion to the party's strength in the country as a whole, as demonstrated, for instance, by the results of parliamentary elections. Late in 1947 Arthur Deakin, Bevin's successor as secretary of the Transport and General Workers, issued a preliminary warning, as did Morgan Phillips, the secretary of the Labour Party[1]; and these admonitions began to have some effect after the Communist *coup* in Czechoslovakia in February of the following year and the international tension in the spring and summer arising from the Berlin blockade. Then in the autumn a remarkable example took place of the embarrassment which a union might suffer if one of its principal officials was a Communist.

The National Union of Mineworkers was supporting the Labour Government, although Communist influence was strong among the officials of its Scottish and Welsh areas; and its executive had consequently decided to support the implementation of the Marshall Plan. Its general secretary, since 1946, however, was a Communist – none other than Arthur Horner, whose earlier difficulties with the party have already been recounted.[2] In spite of these tribulations of his youth, Horner had remained in the party, and he was now prepared to do all he could to swing his union into support of the new Cominform 'line'. Attending a conference of French trade unions in October 1948, he pledged the British miners' support for the French miners' strike, in spite of the fact that this was political action designed to damage the operation of the Marshall Plan.[3]

Horner's statement was at once publicly repudiated by Will Lawther, the President of the union, who sided with the majority of the executive in supporting the Labour Government. After a brisk exchange of repartee between the two leaders in statements in the press, in the course of which Lawther described Horner as 'plain daft',[4] the union executive passed a resolution which declared:

[1] *The Times*, 15 and 22 Dec. 1947.   [2] See above, pp. 58-61.
[3] *The Times*, 14 Oct. 1948.   [4] *Ibid.*, 15 Oct. 1948.

L

The committee in dissociating itself from the unauthorised action of the secretary wishes to make it plain that a recurrence of such conduct will not be tolerated.[1]

This did not prevent the Scottish and Welsh leaders from issuing statements in support of the French miners; and the Scottish area executive went so far as to levy its members a shilling each in order to send a practical token of its solidarity across the Channel.[2]

Meanwhile the majority of the General Council of the T.U.C., which had only one Communist member (Bert Papworth), had decided to take action. At the end of October it issued a statement pointing out that

> Statements made officially by the Communist Party in Britain prove beyond question that sabotage of the European Recovery Programme is its present aim. Communist influences are everywhere at work to frame industrial demands for purposes of political agitation; to magnify industrial grievances; and to bring about stoppages in industry.[3]

A month later it sent out a fuller statement to the unions, entitled *Defend Democracy*, which invited them to consider whether they should take action to prevent Communists from occupying key union posts and from acting as union delegates. It argued that members of the party were engaged in subversive activities and that 'the party centre, which directs the whole of these subversive activities, exists outside the trade union movement'.[4]

This appeal to the unions naturally met with a very varying response, depending upon the extent to which in each individual union Communist strength was already established, and the extent to which the Communist members could convince their non-Communist colleagues that this was a 'witch-hunt' and an infringement of the very principle of democracy which it was supposed to be asserting. A few unions, including the General and Municipal Workers and the National Union of Railwaymen, already had rules to prevent Communists from occupying certain key posts. On the other hand, some other unions, such as the

[1] *The Times*, 29 Oct. 1948.　　[2] *Ibid.*; *Glasgow Herald*, 26 Oct. 1948.
[3] T.U.C. *Report*, 1949, p. 274f.　　[4] *The Times*, 25 Nov. 1948.

Electrical Trades Union and the Fire Brigades Union, were already so fully under Communist control that no effective opposition could be organised, though in the case of the E.T.U. there was an abortive move to found a rival union.[1] The principal conflicts took place in the unions where Communist control was not yet consolidated, but where the party's influence was already strong. Among the larger unions, the obvious cases were the Transport and General Workers and the Amalgamated Engineering Union; among the smaller societies, two examples must suffice – the Clerical and Administrative Workers and the Civil Service Clerical Association.

The Transport and General Workers Union, as we have seen, occupied a key position in Communist strategy owing to the fact that it was the largest of the unions and one in which Communist influence was already strong. Its secretary, Arthur Deakin, however, was a forthright opponent of Communism. The issue was joined at the Biennial Delegate Conference which was held in July 1949. After a vigorous speech by Deakin, the conference endorsed the T.U.C. General Council's policy statement by a majority of over four to one; and a resolution to prevent Communists from holding office in the union was carried by more than two to one.[2] This decision took effect in January 1950, when nine full-time officials were dismissed for Communist sympathies.[3] Among those to go was Bert Papworth, who of course also lost his position on the General Council of the T.U.C.

In the Amalgamated Engineering Union the position was different. There had always been a disproportionately large number of engineering workers in the Communist Party, and this enabled the party to secure a firm foothold in the A.E.U., not so much on the Executive Council – a small body of directly elected representatives – as on the district committees, especially in the London area. In addition, there was a good deal of left-wing feeling among the members which could easily be swung against the T.U.C.'s policy. Consequently, the idea of a ban on Communist office-holders, which would have led to much internal dis-

[1] *Ibid.*, 16 Oct. 1948.   [2] Allen, *Trade Union Leadership*, p. 284.
[3] *Ibid.*, p. 286.

sension, was unanimously rejected by the union's National Committee, although this only contained a minority of Communists.[1] At the same time, the members of the union were solemnly warned of the dangers by their President, Jack Tanner, who after a long career of left-wing activity – he had been at the Second Congress of the Comintern in Moscow in 1920, and had taken a prominent part in the work of the Minority Movement – now came out as a strong opponent of Communism. 'The Communists', he declared,

> look forward to – and work for – the breaking-down of the nation's economy, the weakening of the Labour Movement and the Government.[2]

Thus, although the constitutional situation in the A.E.U. remained unchanged, it was to be expected that in the face of increasing publicity for their activities the Communists would find it difficult to hold their own, still less to make gains, in the contests for union offices.

The Clerical and Administrative Workers Union, like the A.E.U., had a comparatively high proportion of Communists in its membership – high, that is, not absolutely, but in comparison with other unions.[3] Here too they were especially influential in the London and Scottish districts.[4] But the T.U.C. statement rapidly aroused the non-Communists to action, and much of the time of the annual conference at Easter 1949 was devoted to this and kindred matters. The union's affiliation to the National Council of Civil Liberties was terminated, and a resolution was carried to welcome the T.U.C. statement and to adopt the policy that it recommended. This was interpreted to mean that candidates for office in the union should declare whether or not they were Communists, and that in future members of organisations proscribed by the Labour Party should not be allowed to act as delegates to any body with which the union was affiliated.[5] Al-

---

[1] A.E.U., *Report of Proceedings of the National Committee* (1949), p. 300.

[2] *Ibid.*, p. 247.

[3] At the 1949 Congress of the C.P., out of 405 delegates, 85 were members of the A.E.U. and 39 of the C.A.W.U. See *WNV*, xxix, 579.

[4] Fred Hughes, *By Hand and Brain* (1953), p. 143.   [5] *Ibid.*

though the C.A.W.U. was not one of the larger unions, these decisions were a serious setback for the party.

The Civil Service Clerical Association forms a special case, for its members belonged to a profession which was expected to be free of partisan commitments. The union was now affiliated to the T.U.C., and its members were naturally alarmed about the problem of Communist infiltration, at a time when the Government had adopted the policy of removing or transferring civil servants whose loyalty was suspect. The general secretary, L. C. White, had been on the Editorial Board of the *Daily Worker* since 1946,[1] and Communist influence was strong on the executive committee. The union was affiliated to the British-Soviet Friendship Society and the National Council of Civil Liberties; and in 1947-8 a donation of £25 from the union funds was voted for the expenses of a conference organised by the *Daily Worker*. On the other hand, the opponents of Communism had a vocal champion in W. J. Brown, M.P., the former secretary of the union and now its parliamentary secretary.[2] A 'Conference Campaign Committee' came into existence in 1947 or early 1948 – long before the T.U.C. circular – in order to purge the existing executive,[3] and at the annual conference in May 1948 much was done to bring the policy of the union more in line with the views of its members, very few of whom sympathised with the party. A resolution was passed deploring the £25 donation to the *Daily Worker*; affiliation to the British-Soviet Society was terminated; a Communist candidate for the presidency was defeated; and the elections to the executive resulted in a considerable change of political complexion.[4] The conference of a year later continued the same process: the executive elections now resulted in a three-to-one majority against the Communists; affiliation to the National Council of Civil Liberties was also terminated; and the conference endorsed the T.U.C. statement which had been published in the previous November.[5]

---

[1] *DW*, 2 Jan. 1946.
[2] See, e.g., *Parl. Deb.* ser. 5, ccccxl, 296f. (15 July 1947).
[3] *DW*, 9 Jan. 1948.
[4] *The Times*, 26, 27 and 28 May 1948.   [5] *Ibid.*, 26 and 27 May 1949.

The party was thus definitely on the defensive in the unions; and at the Trades Union Congress in September 1949 the General Council received an overwhelming endorsement of its policy by a majority of almost nine to one.[1] Recalcitrant unions could not, of course, be brought to obey the T.U.C. fiat; but trades councils were more vulnerable to pressure from the General Council, which now proceeded to introduce regulations to exclude Communist delegates from the Conference of Trades Councils and its consultative committee.[2] There remained the problem of the London Trades Council: this body, which had a long and distinguished history of activity in metropolitan affairs, had fallen so fully under party control that non-Communist unions had begun to disaffiliate their branches from it. The General Council warned the L.T.C. in 1950 that it must make arrangements to conform to T.U.C. policy[3]; and in 1952, seeing that the warning had had no effect, it decided to disaffiliate the existing body and to form a new London Trades Council free of Communist associations.[4]

With their activities being thus circumscribed, it was difficult for the Communists in the British unions to make much headway in the direction of the principal Cominform objective of the time – the crippling of the European Recovery Programme and the sabotaging of Western re-armament. Nothing to compare with the French political strikes could be arranged, although French Communist union leaders visited Britain to stir the British leaders to similar action. What did occur, however, was a series of unofficial strikes at the London docks and at provincial ports, and there is no doubt that this trouble was fomented and in several cases directly instigated by the party or by Communists from overseas. The Transport section of the Communist-dominated World Federation of Trade Unions had now assumed the role in Soviet global strategy that in the twenties and early thirties had been played by the International of Seamen and Harbour Workers and during one of the British strikes some of its agents attempted to visit the strikers in Britain, but without success.[5]

---

[1] T.U.C. *Report*, 1949, p. 360.   [2] *Ibid.*, 1950, pp. 105f.
[3] *Ibid.*, p. 107.   [4] *Ibid.*, 1952, p. 114.
[5] *Parliamentary Papers*, 1948-9, xxix, 471.

The most serious of the stoppages took place in the spring of 1949, when a number of Canadian ships in British ports were declared 'black' by the Communist-controlled Canadian Seamen's Union, on the pretext of a dispute in which the union was engaged with its Canadian shipowners.[1] Canadian and British Communists co-operated in persuading the dockers not to unload the ships, so as to express their solidarity with the Canadian union. But the trouble could not be maintained indefinitely, and in several cases as soon as the strikers realised that their action was being exploited for the purposes of Cominform strategy, they indicated a desire to resume work.[2]

The success of Communist propaganda in the first instance was due to the genuine grievances of the dockers, both about the working of the Dock Labour Scheme and about the functioning of union machinery. These grievances could not be eliminated overnight; and in the meantime Communist agitation, if not too blatantly political in tone, continued to cause trouble at the docks. Thus, the strike at the London Docks in April 1950 was led by an unofficial Portworkers' Committee which had several Communist members[3]; and the stoppage at the Salford Docks in the spring of 1951 was led by a Communist and was actively supported by the Manchester and Salford Area Committee of the party.[4] By this time the Communist grip on the Transport and General Workers Union had been broken, and in the transport industry the party was adopting an attitude which, with its constant militancy and its enthusiasm for unofficial committees, was closely parallel to its policy in the days of 'Class Against Class'.

*   *   *

There were a good many ways in which the period after 1947

[1] For accounts of this strike see 'Review of the British Dock Strikes, 1949', *Parliamentary Papers*, 1948-9, xxix, 447-94; T. G. McManus, 'Death of a Strike', *Transport and General Workers Record*, xxx (1951), p. 236.

[2] *Parliamentary Papers*, 1948-9, xxix, 461.

[3] 'Unofficial Stoppages in the London Docks', *Parliamentary Papers*, 1950-1, xvi, 145.

[4] 'Report on Certain Aspects of the Manchester (Salford) Dock Strike', *Parliamentary Papers*, 1950-1, xvi, pp. 106, 119.

seemed to be a reversion to the sectarianism of twenty years before. There was the same cutting of ties with the Labour Left,
even with such close associates of recent years as Konni Zilliacus,
who now offended by supporting Tito[1]; there was the same direct
clash with T.U.C. policy, which resulted in the union 'purges',
many of them successfully carried through; and there was the
same attempt to build up a factory organisation of the party –
once again a difficult proposition, beginning as it did after several
years of reversion to a residential basis for party activity.[2] There
was also once more a tendency to abandon the appearance of
'Social-Democratic' methods of election in the party: the choice
of Executive Committee, for instance, which in 1944 and 1945
had been effected by open ballot, reverted in 1947 to ballot with
recommended list, and later – apparently in 1952 – to a system of
open voting for or against a list drawn up by a 'Panels Commission'.[3] This last method was the crudest form of dictation from
above, for the list was in fact drawn up, not by the Panels
Commission nor even by the Executive Committee itself, but by
the Political Committee.[4] From 1943 until 1947 national and
District Congresses were so far as possible held annually; but then
it was decided that once every two years would be often enough
as each Congress needed such elaborate 'preparation'.[5] Finally,
and perhaps most significantly, in 1952 it was decided that the
rank-and-file no longer needed the right to 'take part in the
formulation of party policy', and for this was substituted the much
more limited right to 'take part in the discussion' of policy.[6]

But the position of the party was in many ways less difficult
than in 1929-32. For one thing, it was about ten times as large as
it had then been, and as we have seen it had obtained an almost
unshakeable grip on the management of several trade unions, and
a considerable influence in others. It also had numerous intellec-

---

[1] 'Strong threads link Zilliacus with the Belgrade espionage gang'. *For a
Lasting Peace, for a People's Democracy!* 30 Dec. 1949.

[2] *WNV*, xxix, 27. See also the comments of P. Kerrigan, National Industrial
Organiser, at the 1952 Congress, *WNV*, xxxii, 200.

[3] CP., *Report of the Commission on Inner Party Democracy*, pp. 18f.

[4] *Ibid.*, p. 55.   [5] *WNV*, xxvii, 514.

[6] *Communist Review*, vii (1952), 215.

tuals in its ranks, who were able to provide a constant barrage of propaganda to rally the ranks of the working-class membership. And, further, there was the encouragement afforded by the expanding sphere of Communist control abroad: in 1949 the Chinese Communist Party was at last victorious in its long struggle with the forces of Chiang Kai Shek, and in January 1950 the Communist régime was recognised by the British Government. At the same time, in accordance with its propaganda for 'national independence', the party was endeavouring to assert the truly indigenous character of its own policy: its new long-term programme was called 'The British Road to Socialism', and spoke of a conquest of power through parliamentary means, and a transformation of the British Empire into a 'fraternal association'.[1] It was 'slanderous', said Pollitt, to suggest that the party believed in creating Soviets in Britain.[2]

There was also the fact that, all things considered, the party was now being dealt with very mildly by its opponents. From the middle of 1950 onwards, British troops were committed to battle in Korea against Communist forces, and a case could easily have been made out for suppressing the British party on the ground that it was assisting the King's enemies. For its members not only expounded the North Korean version of the outbreak of the war: they also took their accounts of the campaign from a correspondent on the North Korean side, Alan Winnington of the *Daily Worker*. Winnington interviewed British prisoners of war, and secured messages from them which the party was able to pass on to the next of kin, not without exploitation for the purposes of political propaganda. It was only to be expected under these circumstances that the British party would give credence and wide publicity to the atrocity stories about the conduct of the allied forces, and especially to the charge that germ warfare had been employed by the American air force.[3]

Fortunately for the party members in Britain, there was no

---

[1] The programme was adopted in January 1951. *WNV*, xxxi, 47.

[2] *WN*, ii, 946. This remark pointed the contrast with the party's 1935 programme, which was entitled *For Soviet Britain*.

[3] *WNV*, xxxii, 157 for Executive Committee statement on germ warfare.

general persecution of Communists such as took place in the United States. There were a few isolated cases of what might be regarded as political discrimination: for example, Andrew Rothstein, who held an appointment as a lecturer in Russian History at the London School of Slavonic Studies, was dismissed on grounds of 'inadequate scholarship'; and in Middlesex, where Communist influence had become strong in the local section of the National Union of Teachers, the County Council instituted a ban on the appointment of Communist head teachers.[1] In the civil service, where Communist infiltration could be directly prejudicial to national security, the removal of Communists was effected by transfer rather than by dismissal. Convincing evidence came to light in 1951 of Communist activity in key posts, notably by the cases of the scientists Klaus Fuchs and Bruno Pontecorvo, and by the mystery of the 'missing diplomats' Guy Burgess and Donald MacLean. But no 'witch-hunting' tendencies like those of the Un-American Activities Committee developed in Britain. Although there were institutional reasons for the contrast with the United States in this respect, and although the Korean War necessarily had a greater impact on American opinion than on British, owing to the size of the American forces involved, the situation reflected a widespread – perhaps unduly complacent – feeling in Britain that Scotland Yard and M.I.5 had already effectively taken the measure of the Communist Party, and that the existing precautions, as tightened up by the Labour Government, were the best that could be done.

All the same, as might be expected, the party lost ground during the years of the 'two camps', and especially in the period of the Korean War. In 1947-8, when the new policy was originated, the membership had at last begun to increase once more, perhaps owing to a certain disillusionment in left-wing circles with the performance of the Labour Government. In June 1947 the total was 38,579; by May 1948 it had risen to about 43,000.[2] There was also a revival of the Y.C.L., which now numbered some 3,350.[3] This success encouraged a sense of optimism in the

---

[1] A. Tropp, *The School Teachers* (1957), p. 265.
[2] *WNV*, xxviii, 99.   [3] *Ibid.*, p. 291.

party which was further buoyed up by the completion of the new *Daily Worker* building and press in Farringdon Street in 1948.[1] One of the most optimistic of all was William Rust, who had now saddled the party with a press that was to prove uneconomic for a paper with so small a circulation. But the general enthusiasm did not disappear even after Rust's sudden death from a heart attack in 1949. It was decided to fight a hundred constituencies at the forthcoming General Election – almost four times as many as had ever been put up before. The result was disastrous: Both Gallacher and Piratin, the sitting members, were defeated, and as the 'crypto-Communists' also disappeared, the party was deprived of representation in Parliament for the first time since 1935. Only three of the hundred candidates – the two retiring M.P.s and Pollitt at Rhondda East – polled enough votes to save their deposits; and at £150 each for its other contests, the party thus made a contribution of £14,550 directly to the Treasury.

After this, the real decline in the influence of the party had to be admitted. Communist bookshops all over the country were being forced to close for lack of custom, and the *Daily Worker* readership and advertising revenue slumped heavily.[2] The membership total began to fall once more and by the end of 1952 was less than 36,000.[3] At the 1951 General Election the leadership naturally decided to concentrate its efforts on a much smaller number of constituencies, and this time only ten candidates were put up. But even these candidates mostly lost votes by comparison with 1950, and not one of them saved his deposit. It was a miserable outcome for a party which only seven years before had been expecting to play a prominent role in post-war Britain.

[1] Rust, *Story of the Daily Worker*, pp. 126f.
[2] *WNV*, xxx, 303 and 453.   [3] *WNV*, xxxiii, 88.

CHAPTER X

AFTER STALIN:
EXIT OF THE INTELLECTUALS

ONE of the remarkable features of the Communist Party in the later nineteen-forties was the way in which it kept a core of strength among the intellectuals who had joined it in the 'Popular Front' period. Since many of them were individuals of considerable talent and ability, who should have been capable of arriving at some estimate of what was really happening in Russia, non-Communists were led to believe that these intellectual members of the party were completely cynical and devoid of all respect for the elementary rights of citizenship. The events of the middle nineteen-fifties, however, showed that this assumption was largely incorrect. The Communist intelligentsia, it appeared, were not so much hard-hearted as hot-headed: and it was their intelligence after all that was at fault, rather than their basic good intentions.

The crumbling of support for the party among the members of the professions was not a sudden affair, but a gradual realisation of the tyranny of the Stalinist system. It may appear paradoxical that this realisation was effected only by the manifestations of crisis that surrounded the decline and death of the tyrant himself. But previously, of course, there had been the menace of Fascism and the years of war, which went far to provide a justification in the minds of many observers for the harsh measures of 'Soviet justice'.

To those who believed in the merits of Communist rule the regimentation of scientific and cultural thought in the post-war years presented some awkward problems of explanation. This was particularly exemplified in what became known as the 'Lysenko affair'. It was in 1946-7 that Lysenko first achieved international prominence by his criticisms of the orthodox theory of genetics.[1] He was a plant-breeder with some practical successes behind him, but these afforded no justification for an attempt to overthrow the work of Weismann, Mendel and Morgan, who had made a science out of the subject in the course of the preceding century. Leading geneticists in Britain, when they heard of the prominence that Lysenko was attaining, at once took umbrage, and the few of them who were members of the Communist Party were less willing to defend Lysenko's views than to maintain that he had a right to express them. Dr John Lewis, the editor of the *Modern Quarterly*, a party journal, was in 1947 willing to concede that

> British geneticists agree with a considerable body of Russian geneticists in passing severe criticism on Lysenko's work.[2]

So far, it is evident, the issue had placed no great strain on the political loyalty of Communist geneticists in Britain: for it seemed that Lysenko's claims, although prominently expressed, were not yet accepted in Russia to the exclusion of other views. Unfortunately, however, the Lysenko notions of environmental influence on heredity tied in well with Marxist theory; and as a result their sponsor was encouraged to erect his ideas into a new orthodoxy. The climax of this process was reached at a meeting of the Soviet Academy of Agricultural Sciences in August 1948, when his scientific opponents were expelled from the Presidium of the Academy.

Not long after this, a B.B.C. discussion took place, in which several non-Communist geneticists made forthright attacks on Lysenko, while J. B. S. Haldane, in reply, gained some debating advantage by refusing to commit himself until he had seen the official report of the Soviet Academy meeting, which was not yet available in Britain.[3] Up to this point, it seems, the Communist geneticists in Britain, although unhappy about the situation facing their colleagues in Russia, had no specially strong reason for reconsidering their own political affiliations. But there now devel-

---

[1] For an introduction to the controversy, see J. Langdon Davies, *Russia Puts the Clock Back* (1949)

[2] *Modern Quarterly*, ii, 352.   [3] Printed in the *Listener*, xl, 873-5.

oped an attempt by the leaders of the British party to secure an endorsement of Lysenko's views by their own scientific members. One party geneticist later declared:

> The first thing that infuriated me was an article in the *Daily Worker* by Clemens Dutt, reviewing a book by Lysenko and attacking the orthodox geneticists. This at a time when Haldane, the leading party scientist and geneticist, was refusing to commit himself.[1]

According to this source, the party then called a meeting of its geneticists – about a dozen of them – but found them in opposition to the Lysenko 'line'. This did not deter the *Daily Worker* from publishing an article by a party official, Emile Burns, attacking orthodox genetics.[2] Haldane, who was still the chairman of the *Daily Worker* board, was forced to resort to the method of circulating a cyclostyled reply.

There followed a meeting of the Engels Society, a scientific discussion group associated with the party's Cultural Committee, at which apparently 'tempers ran quite high'.[3] Then in February 1949 a two-day 'school' on the controversy was held, without however resolving the bitter differences within the party. Finally, Haldane publicly stated his disagreement with Lysenko in an article in the *Modern Quarterly*,[4] and withdrew from active work for the party. He declared that he was still in agreement with the party's policy on a range of political issues, but his regular *Daily Worker* series of articles on scientific topics, which had been one of the main attractions of the paper, now came to an end. Several other geneticists also left the party at about the same time. There were, however, a few scientists who managed to swallow the Lysenko 'line', notably the botanist James Fyfe, who in 1950 published a little book entitled *Lysenko is Right* – without, however, any reference to the criticisms made by Haldane. His loyalty, like that of Klugmann, was soon outmoded by events: by January 1957 an official party delegation on its return from Russia

---

[1] Quoted in G. A. Almond (ed.), *The Appeals of Communism* (Princeton, 1954), p. 314. For the article, see *DW*, 17 Nov. 1948.
[2] *DW*, 30 Dec. 1948.   [3] Almond, *op. cit.*, p. 316.
[4] 'In Defence of Genetics', *Modern Quarterly*, iv, 194-202.

could admit that 'For ten years it was impossible to carry out genuinely scientific work in the field of genetics'.[1]

The Lysenko affair had only a limited direct impact in Britain, for few of the party members could follow the scientific intricacies of the controversy, and those who were not experts in the subject tended to give the benefit of their own ignorance to the new Soviet 'line'. At the same time, it was an indication of a general threat to freedom of thought, which involved the establishment of a party orthodoxy of view in every sphere, whether in the sciences or in the arts. The intellectuals, who after all had the most to lose if any such orthodoxy were established in Britain, must have suffered a good many twinges of conscience as they read of the growing regimentation of their counterparts in Russia under the orders of Zhdanov. Yet even more serious evidence of tyranny in Russia and Eastern Europe was to come to light in the last year of Stalin's long period of rule.

*　　*　　*

It was in November 1952 that the Slansky trial in Czechoslovakia brought into real prominence the recrudescence of anti-semitism in Eastern Europe. For the British Communists, many of whom were of Jewish origin, it was of only incidental importance that the principal defendant, Slansky, was a leader in whom Pollitt had as recently as 1948 declared his utmost confidence: after all, the same thing had happened in an even more obvious fashion over Tito. What mattered was that of the fourteen defendants in the trial, eleven were Jews, and the indictment included a denunciation of 'Joint' (the Joint Distribution Committee, a Zionist charitable organisation) as an agency of 'imperialist' espionage. The suspicions of anti-semitism which this trial re-awoke were speedily reinforced in January 1953 by the news from Moscow of the arrest of a number of Russian Jewish doctors, on a charge of plotting to assassinate Stalin – again, on the instructions of the supposedly sinister 'Joint'.

The impact of these events on the British party membership clearly worried its leaders. Pollitt had to explain the situation very

[1] *WN*, iv, 39.

carefully: the Zionist movement, he said, had always been 'a tool of British imperialism'; now it was 'increasingly shifting its allegiance to the stronger American imperialism', and the new state of Israel had become 'a pawn of the U.S.A.'. Zionism, he declared, was therefore 'a ready-made tool and weapon for the American-backed spies, traitors and wreckers'.[1] Mick Bennett, the national organiser, who was himself of Jewish origin, attempted to divert the charge of anti-semitism to the Western powers by maintaining that 'support for Zionism and support for anti-semitism often go hand in hand'.[2] It was certainly fortunate for the Communist Parties of the West that the Rosenberg appeal – to save a Jewish couple sentenced to death for espionage in the United States – could be played up at this time with the intention of deflecting the charges of anti-semitism away from the Communist régimes.[3]

The outcome of the affair of the Jewish doctors, although it resulted in their rehabilitation, was not such as to re-assure any Communist who was concerned about the processes of Soviet justice. It turned out that the affair was simply one move in a gigantic struggle for the succession to Stalin, whose death took place in March 1953. The paeans of praise had hardly ceased to sound at the dictator's funeral when the charges against the doctors were withdrawn and their prosecutor arrested – a patent act of justice which naturally caused considerable embarrassment to Communists who had steadfastly defended the original accusations. Three months later Beria, who was in charge of the Russian 'security forces', was removed from office and placed on trial for treason. The indictment, published in December, accused him of a catalogue of crimes including murder, sabotage and treason.

After this, the comparatively slow decline of Malenkov's position of authority and his resignation from the office of Prime Minister in 1955 seemed at least to suggest a relaxation of the

---

[1] WNV, xxxiii, 5.   [2] Ibid., p.114.

[3] A. H. Hanson, Reader in Public Administration at Leeds University, who left the party on this issue, later pointed out that the campaign was 'proclaiming the Rosenbergs' innocence of activities which from a Communist point of view are highly meritorious'. New Reasoner, Autumn 1957, p. 81.

TWENTIETH NATIONAL CONGRESS, MARYLEBONE, FEBRUARY 1948

grim tension that prevailed in Moscow just before and after Stalin's death. There followed the visit of Bulganin and Krushchev to Yugoslavia in the spring of 1955, which involved an astonishing admission of culpability by the Russian leaders for their country's earlier hostility towards Tito's régime. Non-Communists, who had long since accepted the fact that Stalin was ruthless in the use of his power, could see a ray of hope in these new developments – hope that the dictatorship might be giving way to a more broadly based system of control. But those members of the British party who still believed in the existence of 'Soviet democracy' and in the 'fraternity of Socialist nations' were now growing seriously disquieted. It was becoming more and more obvious that correct judicial forms had not in the past been observed in Soviet trials, and although there was little direct news of the condition of Russian Jewry, what there was was not encouraging. The intellectuals converted to Communism in the 'red decade', who had stayed in the party ever since, were now at last being pushed towards an 'agonising reappraisal' of their reasons for belonging to the party.

*   *   *

It is against this background of rising discontent with 'Stalinism' that we can study the impact on British Communism of the shattering events of 1956.[1] The Twentieth Congress of the Communist Party of the Soviet Union was held in February, and Pollitt, Dutt and George Matthews, who were the representatives of the British party, were present to hear Krushchev speak of the probability that in the future 'forms of transition to Socialism will become more and more diversified'.[2] This in itself implied a relaxation of the international discipline of the Communist movement, and was the logical concomitant of the attack on the 'cult of personality' which was now given official sanction by the Russian party. But the delegates of the foreign Communist parties were apparently not admitted to the secret session of the Russian party

[1] In preparing this section I have found useful an article by G. W. Grainger, 'Chaos in the British C.P.', *Problems of Communism*, vi, 2, pp. 8–14.
[2] *For a Lasting Peace, for a People's Democracy!* 17 Feb. 1956.

M

at which Krushchev made sensational revelations about the
Stalinist terror of the 1930s. They learned merely that the speech
had been made, and may have gathered some of the details of its
contents. It was evidently the intention of the Russian leadership
to break the news of Stalin's 'errors' very gradually, both to the
rank and file of their own party and to their supporters in foreign
countries.

The next Congress of the British party took place in April,
before the rank and file could obtain much idea of the unpublished Krushchev speech. A general impression of its 'line', however, was given to the delegates by Pollitt at a speech delivered in
a secret session. Pollitt spoke of 'confessions of guilt made under
pressure', and referred also to errors made by Stalin in the course
of the war.[1] He announced the British party's acceptance of the
new Russian attitude to Yugoslavia, in words which have already
been quoted.[2] Pollitt's exposition must have taken many of the
delegates by surprise: some of them may even have thought that
their legs were being pulled, especially as the secret session was
held on 1st April. At any rate, the fresh information seemed to
raise more questions than it answered, and it was natural that the
Congress should pass a resolution regretting that the Russian
party had not yet published the text of the Krushchev speech.[3]

Although a few sharp words of reproof were spoken in the
course of the Congress debates, the impact of the news from
Russia was too sudden to result in the formulation of any demand
for reform inside the party while the Congress was sitting. But
after it had dispersed, mutterings of criticism began to grow
louder, both in the British party and throughout the whole
Communist world; and the British leadership realised that they
must needs trim the ship in order to ride out the storm. Dutt,
who had made what seemed an offensively complacent comment
in the May issue of his *Labour Monthly* – speaking of Stalin's
errors as mere 'spots on the sun' which 'would only startle an
inveterate Mithras-worshipper'[4] was severely taken to task even

[1] *WN*, iii, 246.   [2] See above, p. 152.
[3] The resolution was only revealed on 21 June. See *DW*, 22 June 1956.
[4] *Labour Monthly*, xxxviii, 194.

by his closest colleagues, and was obliged to assume an attitude of concern.[1] Pollitt, who had recently been making long journeys abroad ostensibly in search of better health, now felt it wise to retire from the secretaryship: he was replaced by John Gollan, a native of the Edinburgh slums, who had been a party official for over twenty years and had been marked out for the succession after the death of Rust. Pollitt now became chairman of the party, and Gallacher, the existing chairman, was 'kicked' even further 'upstairs' to the new post of President. The Executive Committee now admitted that in the past 'on the basis of false information we, in all good faith, made a number of mistakes'. It sought to anticipate some of the criticisms of its own supporters by acknowledging 'a certain dogmatism, rigidity and sectarianism' in its own behaviour.[2] To put matters right, a 'Commission on Inner Party Democracy' was set up to consider ways of developing democracy inside the party; and it was also agreed to revise the party's programme, 'The British Road to Socialism', in order to ensure that it contained safeguards against the infringement of democratic liberty and 'Socialist legality'.

But there were plenty of Communists, both in Britain and abroad, who felt that an even more searching enquiry was necessary into the reasons for the 'errors' of the past. Attacking the British leadership, Edward Thompson, an extra-mural lecturer at Leeds University, pointed out that the plea of 'false information' was not an adequate excuse for an 'uncritical and inaccurate propaganda about the Soviet Union, extending over a period of twenty years'.[3] His letter was printed in the *Daily Worker* on the very day which saw the publication of the secret Krushchev speech by the U.S. Department of State – a shattering event for the Communist parties of Western Europe, which at first seemed to threaten their very existence. Within a fortnight Togliatti, the Italian Communist leader, was going beyond the attacks on Stalin and calling for a wider study of the reasons for the 'degeneration' of Soviet society, as he put it.[4] A few days

[1] *Ibid.*, p. 249; *DW*, 23 May 1956.   [2] *DW*, 16 May 1956.
[3] *DW*, 4 June 1956.   [4] Togliatti, *Questions Posed by the Twentieth Congress* (published by *World News*, 1956), p. 3.

later the Political Committee of the British party issued a statement accepting the State Department text of the Krushchev
speech as authentic, and agreeing with Togliatti that 'it will be
necessary to make a profound Marxist analysis of the causes of the
degeneration in the functioning of Soviet democracy and party
democracy'.[1] These criticisms, however, seemed to threaten the
whole Soviet system and in particular might undermine the
position of the new Soviet leaders. The latter therefore acted
swiftly to call a halt to the scope of the enquiry. A statement was
published by the Central Committee of the Russian party which
took Togliatti to task for referring to the 'degeneration' of Soviet
society. The statement quoted with approval other remarks of
Togliatti to the effect that 'the essence of the Socialist system has
not been lost. . . . This society has retained its basic democratic
character.'[2]

From this point onward the bounds of the controversy, so far
as it affected Russia, seemed to have been clearly laid down. In
July, Pollitt, Gollan and Bert Ramelson visited Moscow for talks
with Krushchev and others of the Russian hierarchy[3]: they no
doubt received some vigorous advice on how far they could go
in criticism. Certainly on their return the party's official attitude
became once more very cautious. The rules of 'democratic
centralism' were kept in operation, but a safety-valve of discussion had already been opened in the party press and this was
retained for the time being. The demand of a number of branches
for a special Congress with full powers was not acceded to, but
it was decided to hold a National Conference, at which the
various issues might at least be ventilated. Finally, the membership of the Commissions on Inner Party Democracy and on the
party programme was extended, though there was still to be a
preponderance of full-time officials on both.[4] The editor of the
Daily Worker was allowed to admit, in a note of comment
attached to a letter of shocked enquiry from Professor Hyman

[1] DW, 22 June 1956.
[2] Resolution of 30 June, reprinted in The Anti-Stalin Campaign and
International Communism (ed. Russian Institute, Columbia University, New
York, 1956, p. 300.   [3] DW, 11 July 1956.   [4] DW, 16 July 1956.

Levy and others, that the charges of anti-semitic persecution in Russia were 'essentially correct'[1]; but no further airing of the matter was permitted, pending further investigations.

It soon became evident, however, that the tide of resentment among the rank and file of the party was still rising. Already in July Edward Thompson, together with John Saville, an economics lecturer at the University of Hull, had launched a cyclostyled journal entitled the 'Reasoner', the first issue of which contained a high critical article on the functioning of 'democratic centralism' in the British party. The editors at once began to receive large numbers of letters from sympathisers and well-wishers within the party. The Yorkshire District Committee endeavoured to assert the party discipline by urging them to cease publication, but they refused, and the matter was referred to the party centre.[2] In September a second issue of the journal was published, just as the Political Committee sent instructions to the editors to close down. The issue contained articles by Professor Levy, by Doris Lessing, the novelist, and by Ronald Meek, the economist. The editors inserted a note to say that they did not propose to submit unless they received 'adequate guarantees that means will be found whereby minority views in the Communist Party can be fully posed, developed and sustained'. Perhaps without realising it, the editors had already passed from a Leninist to a liberal position, which was exemplified by their use of a quotation from Diderot:

> Though a lie may serve for the moment, it is inevitably injurious in the long run; the truth, on the other hand, inevitably serves in the end even if it may hurt for the moment.[3]

★   ★   ★

Meanwhile, Eastern Europe was experiencing severe repercussions arising from 'de-Stalinisation'; and as unrest there rose to a sudden climax in the late autumn, fresh blows were struck at the stability of the already shaky British party. The Poznan riots in July were an unpleasant curtain-raiser for dramatic events in Poland, and the *dénouement* in October, with its revelation of a

[1] *DW*, 3 Aug. 1956.   [2] *WN*, iii, 600.   [3] 'Reasoner', Sept. 1956, p. 21.

long history of Russian interference in Polish internal politics, provided cold comfort for Communists steeped in illusions about the voluntary co-operation of nations in the Soviet bloc. Then on 23rd October came the outbreak of the Hungarian Revolution, and in the next two weeks the world witnessed the spectacle of workers and students overturning an established Communist régime, only to succumb to the counter-revolutionary intervention of the Red Army.

In this crisis the bankruptcy of the British party leadership's judgment became rapidly evident: after all, Rakosi, who was the principal villain of the piece, was one of Pollitt's heroes.[1] On 25th October the *Daily Worker* described the uprising as a 'counter-revolution', and George Matthews, who was acting as editor while Campbell was away in Russia, refused to publish the dispatches of the paper's special correspondent in Hungary, Peter Fryer, who on 27th October started sending vivid details of what was going on. There were immediate ructions in the *Daily Worker* offices: about a third of the staff resigned their jobs, including Malcolm MacEwen, the features editor, and J. Friell, better known as 'Gabriel', who had been the paper's cartoonist for over twenty years.[2] The party officials made desperate efforts to divert the attention of the membership to the Suez crisis, which reached its climax at about the same time: but it was to little avail. Soon reports of membership resignations began to accumulate: three prominent trade unionists, Jack Grahl and Leo Keely of the Fire Brigades Union, and Les Cannon of the E.T.U., wrote to Gollan urging a dissolution of the party[3]; John Horner, the secretary of the Fire Brigades Union, and Alex Moffat, an official of the Scottish Miners, sent in their resignations,[4] and those of Grahl, Keely and Cannon speedily followed.[5] Thus at one blow the party lost its control of the Fire Brigades Union; and the defection of Les Cannon threatened its grip in the E.T.U., for he had been the head of the union training college. There were also reports of rank-and-file miners' demonstrations against Com-

[1] See above, p. 149.   [2] *Manchester Guardian*, 16 Nov. 1956.
[3] *The Times*, 15 Nov. 1956.   [4] *Ibid.*, 14 Nov. 1956.
[5] *Manchester Guardian*, 15 Nov. 1956.

munism in Scotland and South Wales. Stirlingshire and Lanark-shire pit workers travelled to Edinburgh in an attempt to force the resignation of the remaining party members among their leaders, and union lodges in South Wales passed resolutions with a similar purport. In neither case, however, did the entrenched Communist officials give way.[1]

But if the party suffered sudden and serious defections in the industrial sphere, this was not so grave a problem as that pre-sented by the revolt of the intellectual members of the party. It is reasonable to suppose that they provided many of the individual resignations, the total of which, according to Gollan's admission, had reached 590 by early December.[2] To stem the exodus, the Executive Committee at last agreed to the demand for a special Congress. At the same time, it suspended Thompson and Saville from membership of the party, after they had produced a third issue of the 'Reasoner' strongly denouncing the Soviet action in Hungary.[3] Thompson and Saville promptly resigned from the party[4]; but there were other intellectuals still inside, who could continue to embarrass the leadership. An impressive group wrote a joint letter to the *Daily Worker* criticising the party's policy over Hungary. The letter was refused publication, and the group thereupon sent it to *Tribune* and the *New Statesman*.[5] Its appearance brought a severe censure from the Political Committee on the authors, who included Eric Hobsbawm, the chairman of the Historians' Group, Christopher Hill, the well-known Marxist historian of the Civil War, and Professor Hyman Levy, who was just back from a harrowing investigation of anti-semitism in Russia.[6]

Meanwhile, the party's 'line' on the Hungarian events was being debated by the branches: and for the first time since 1929, it was obvious that the lead from the party centre was really being challenged at the local level. By the middle of December

[1] *The Times*, 27 Nov. and 5 Dec. 1956.
[2] *Manchester Guardian*, 11 Dec. 1956.
[3] *WN*, iii, 726. [4] *The Times*, 15 Nov. 1956.
[5] *Tribune*, 30 Nov. and *New Statesman*, 1 Dec. 1956.
[6] *WN*, iii, 781. For Levy's report of his investigations into Russian anti-semitism, especially during the 'Black Years' 1948-52, see *WN*, iv, 20-3.

the voting figures were: in favour of the executive's policy, 3582; against, 1080; abstentions, 414.[1] These figures encouraged the potential opposition leaders – mostly journalists and university dons – to hope for a transformation of policy at the Party Congress, which was now scheduled for Easter 1957. But they soon realised that there was comparatively little that they could do: the old rules of 'democratic centralism' saw to that. Malcolm MacEwen, for instance, arranged to speak to the Uxbridge Borough membership, but Gollan at once pointed out to the Borough Secretary that this was contrary to rule, and the meeting was cancelled.[2] Peter Fryer quickly wrote a small book about his experiences in Hungary, and also went round addressing public meetings: as a result, he was 'summarily expelled' from the party by the London District Committee.[3]

The only rallying point that presented itself for the 'opposition of the intellectuals' was a Minority Report of the Commission on Inner Party Democracy, which, together with the Majority Report, was presented to the Executive Committee in December. The Minority, consisting of Christopher Hill, Malcolm MacEwen and Peter Cadogan, a school teacher, deplored the fact that their colleagues on the Commission consisted almost entirely of full-time officials of the party. They regretted that the Commission had not been able to probe more fully into the faults of party structure, and that the evidence which they had had time to consider was comparatively limited in scope. At the same time, they made a number of highly significant criticisms: they maintained that 'democratic centralism', of the type that Lenin considered suitable for a revolutionary organisation, was not appropriate 'to our party or to present British conditions'.[4] They pointed out that the real power in the party rested with the Political Committee, which in effect chose the members of the Executive Committee by drawing up a list of recommended candidates which was accepted without question by the Executive Committee and the

[1] *DW*, 17 Dec. 1956.
[2] CP, *Report of the Commission on Inner Party Democracy* (1957), pp. 59f.
[3] P. Fryer, *Hungarian Tragedy* (1956); *Manchester Guardian*, 24 Dec. 1956.
[4] *Report on Inner Party Democracy*, pp. 46f.

Panels Commission. They attacked the existing limitations on free discussion inside the party, as exemplified by the Uxbridge affair; and, apparently in an effort to mobilise support at the special Congress, they inserted a demand for the removal of party leaders who were unwilling to abandon 'outworn and discredited policies and methods inherited from the past'.[1]

The Majority Report was signed by the other twelve members of the Commission, of whom only two were not full-time officials of the party. In contrast to the Minority, they held relentlessly to the Leninist position. They appealed to the parallel provided by trade union structure:

> That the common interest demands that factional groupings be not permitted, that there should be one, not two or many, centres of leadership, that journals be controlled by the organisation concerned and not by self-appointed individuals, that discipline and unity in action are essential, that splinter tactics and breakaways mean splitting the front – all this is widely accepted and understood without great difficulty by those with experience of the class struggle, particularly in factory, pit and depot.[2]

The 'cult of the individual' in Russia, they maintained, had come about not as a result of 'democratic centralism', but as a result of the 'violation of the practices of democratic centralism'. Their proposals for change were therefore limited to minor recommendations such as the extension of 'pre-Congress discussion' in the branches and in the party press. They were satisfied with the 'recommended list' system of election, though they suggested that the proportion of full-time officials on the Executive Committee should not be permitted to exceed half. For the rest, they re-affirmed their hostility to the development of 'factions' inside the party, and they declared that 'the responsibility for the development of democratic life in the branches' rested with the Executive and District Committees.[3]

Not very surprisingly, it was the Majority Report which was endorsed by the Executive Committee at its meeting on 16th December: the Minority Report, though circulated for information, was rejected *in toto*. 'When we speak of freedom of dis-

[1] *Ibid.*, p. 59. [2] *Ibid.*, p. 8. [3] *Ibid.*, p. 38.

cussion', said the Executive, 'we do not mean freedom to advocate ideas hostile to the interests of the working class and contrary to the basic principles of Marxism-Leninism.'[1] The Minority also quoted Lenin; but their hostility to 'democratic centralism' seemed to suggest that they really wanted to retreat from Lenin back to Marx – or to an entirely liberal standpoint. If the party was still to be based on Leninism, there was no doubt that the Executive Committee had the logic on its side. Indeed, the intellectuals were involved in considerable mental confusion: they could not really find a basis for their views, except in an abstract 'morality' against which they were supposed to have been immunised by their years of Marxist training. Professor Levy of all people – the author of a number of works on dialectical materialism – had to be reproved by Gollan for speaking of 'morality':

> What has this to do with Marxism and the determining of a class position on events? The moral estimation flows from, and cannot be separated from, the political estimation.[2]

But the test that was to come, at the Congress at Easter, 1957, was not so much a test of logic as of existing party machinery. What with the representation of the Executive and of the District Committees, Congress was always heavily weighted in the direction of the official 'line'. Could the unrest of the rank and file break through the obstacles that stood in the way? It seemed doubtful.

*   *   *

The national press was astir to see what would happen at the Easter Congress of the party, and we have numerous accounts of the scene at the Hammersmith Town Hall where it was meeting. Outside the hall, critics of the party leadership assembled to pass round leaflets and to paint slogans such as 'Sack Harry!', while inside the more than six hundred delegates spent four days in sharp debates – an experience unexampled since the foundation of the party. Gollan's political report, delivered on the first day, provoked some controversy. He admitted that, owing to the

[1] *Report on Inner Party Democracy*, p. iv.   [2] *WN*, iv, 154.

growth of 'revisionism' as he put it, some 7,000 members had left the party in 1956, reducing its total membership to 27,000; but he declared, with exasperating complacency, 'They are not our best comrades, otherwise they would not have left.'[1] This point was later taken up by Alick West, one of the intellectuals, who mourned the party's loss of such able members as Doris Lessing and Edward Thompson.[2]

A number of amendments to Gollan's report were debated, but when it came to the voting the rebel element proved to be very small. It was evident that the old hands had done their best to 'pack' the Congress with their supporters: the average age of the delegates with full powers was 40, as against 34 in 1956; and the proportion of them with over fifteen years' membership rose from 31 per cent to 47 per cent.[3] In spite of this, however, a number of highly critical speeches were made. One of the most outspoken opponents of the platform was John McLoughlin, a Dagenham shop steward, who demanded 'at least a partially new front bench'.[4] The only member of the existing Executive to admit to oppositional views was Brian Behan, a building worker, who revealed that he had been against the Soviet intervention in Hungary. His standpoint, however, was voted down 'by an overwhelming majority on a show of hands'.[5] Peter Fryer's appeal against expulsion from the party also aroused little sympathy, and was rejected by 486 to 31.[6]

Although the temper of the Congress was clear by now, there were still some striking attacks on the leadership to come. The climax came on the third day, when Professor Levy reported on his visit to Russia to investigate anti-semitism. In the course of his trip, he said, he saw and heard of things 'that shook me to my foundations – I got my belly full, enough to last me my life.' He posed the question – how much did the British party leaders know of it all, and conceal?

I asked Johnnie Campbell – did he know? I could see the relief on

[1] CP, 25th Congress Report (1957), p. 22.   [2] DW, 22 Apr. 1957.
[3] CP, 24th Congress Resolutions and Proceedings (1956), p. 18; 25th Congress Report, p. 77.
[4] Observer, 21 Apr. 1957.   [5] DW, 22 Apr. 1957.   [6] Ibid.

his face: at last someone was going to talk about it. Johnnie Gollan has sworn to me blankly, hand on heart, that he did not know anything about it. Did Harry Pollitt know?[1]

But Pollitt, who was acting as chairman of the Congress, wisely held his peace; and it was left to Andrew Rothstein on the following day to create a fresh storm by defending the leadership against the 'groups of backboneless and spineless intellectuals who had turned in upon their own emotions and frustrations'. Above the uproar that followed this remark McLoughlin could be heard shouting 'You lying old swine'.[2] But abuse was a poor substitute for voting-cards.

The debate on 'inner-party democracy' was left to the last day of the conference, by which time it was obvious that the Minority Report could not possibly find acceptance. Christopher Hill nevertheless brought forward an amendment in its favour, and spoke with disarming frankness of the crisis of the intellectuals:

> We have been living in a world of illusions. That is why the Twentieth Congress of the Soviet Union and Hungary came as such a shock. We had not been prepared for these events by our leaders. We have lived in a snug little world of our own invention.

Hill did not confine himself to blaming other people:

> Some of us, including myself, have a grave responsibility for having hushed up some of the things we knew.[3]

It was an honest confession, but it could not solve the dilemma: either you were not a Communist at all, or, if you were, you had to accept the need for Leninist discipline, for restrictions on freedom of discussion, and for concealment of the truth. As Mrs Margaret Hunter at once ironically pointed out, the implications of Hill's attitude would lead to 'the creation of some liberal kind of association for the expression of views by experienced individuals or for the protection of people's private consciences'.[4] In the upshot, there were only 23 supporters for the Minority Report, with 472 votes condemning it and 15 abstentions.[5]

---

[1] *The Times*, 22 Apr. 1957.   [2] *DW* and *News Chronicle*, 23 Apr. 1957.
[3] *The Times*, 23 Apr. 1957.   [4] *Ibid.*   [5] *Ibid.*

And so the Congress broke up with the 'old guard' still in full control. All the candidates on the recommended list for the new Executive were elected, and Brian Behan, who had been 'dropped' from the list, had to be content with the position of 'runner-up' in the ballot. Professor Levy was the 'runner-up' for a place on the Appeals Committee, though he received less than a quarter of the vote of any of the successful candidates,[1] It was not without real satisfaction that Pollitt could maintain, in his closing speech, that the Congress had 'cleared the air': he urged the delegates to return to their homes with the intention of getting down at once to 'mass work'.[2]

This injunction was not obeyed by the leading intellectuals. Many of them, including Christopher Hill, now sent in their resignations from the party[3]; some of them found an outlet for further expostulation in new Marxist journals, such as the *Universities and Left Review*, and the *New Reasoner*. Others stayed in the party pending the 1958 registration, and merely dropped out of political activity. The argumentative Professor Levy insisted on having a further word in the *New Statesman* – though it read more like a grudging tribute to the existing leadership than a criticism of them. Gollan, Dutt, and Pollitt, he said,

> are all highly able men who have sacrificed themselves for a cause in which they believe. . . . They regard themselves as the Chosen People, the People of the Book, the personal custodians of a trust that is part of a great international movement. . . . They are time-less, and so they and their bodyguard must always be re-elected. . . . Even if the party membership were to be reduced to nought, they would still remain 'The Party'. Its soul would go marching on.[4]

[1] *DW*, 23 Apr. 1957.   [2] *Ibid.*
[3] *Daily Express*, 11 June 1957.   [4] *New Statesman*, 27 Apr. 1957.

CHAPTER XI

ILLUSION AND REALITY

THE record of the British Communist Party since its foundation has been one of herculean efforts but of tantalising disappointments. In view of the importance of Britain as a world power, the Communists of other countries have set great store by the progress of their British comrades, but their high hopes have never been fulfilled. As Dimitrov is supposed to have put it in the nineteen-thirties, 'Our British movement is a pain: it will not grow, neither will it die.'[1] Compared with the parties of other European countries, it has always remained extraordinarily weak and ineffective: it has never secured the allegiance of a mass following, nor won the trust and co-operation of the major organisations of the labour movement. Its leaders have assumed a tutorial role of some importance in the development of Communism within the old Empire, and particularly in India[2]: but this success only emphasises by contrast the continuity of failure at home. The main reason is readily apparent: throughout the whole period, the British people have never been in revolutionary mood. All the absurdities of the history of the party spring from this one fact, that it has been a revolutionary party in a non-revolutionary situation.

It is not for the inhabitants of Western Europe and North America, whose political structure is at least in part a product of violent change, to condemn the concept of revolution as such. Most of us must agree with Locke that an oppressed people has the right to use the force of arms in order to throw off its

[1] Valtin, *Out of the Night*, p. 321.

[2] For the influence of Dutt and Pollitt on the Indian party in recent years, see Masani, *Communist Party of India*, esp. pp. 108-10 (Dutt's intervention in 1950) and pp. 203-18 (Pollitt's criticisms at the Third Congress at Madurai in 1953-4). But Masani suggests the possibility (pp. 227f.) that the Chinese party may be taking over some of the responsibilities of the British.

oppressors. This makes it difficult to condemn out of hand the twentieth-century revolutionaries, such as those of Russia or China, who have succeeded in overthrowing régimes of tyranny and corruption in their own countries. Nor is there much to be gained, given a revolutionary situation, from an indictment of the thought and teaching of Lenin, who did so much to codify the technique of a successful seizure of power. The faults of Communism lie not with its Russian progenitor, catering as he did primarily for a particular situation in his own country, but with his followers in other countries, where the social and political environment was or is entirely different. Lenin encouraged them in error, of course, by suggesting a universal validity for the solutions that he was propounding for his own immediate problems: but the major responsibility must rest with those who, though actually facing objective circumstances which had no comparison with those in Russia, still attempted to impose on those circumstances an alien code of political action.

If the main reason for the failure of the British party can best be described in this way, we are left with the problem of why those men and women who did join the party – admittedly, a tiny minority of the total population of Britain – were willing to brave the hostility of their fellow-countrymen by associating themselves with its propaganda and devoting so much of their time and efforts to its maintenance. At the outset we must, of course, bear in mind that people drift into political affiliations for a variety of motives, not all of them necessarily associated with a conscious process of political reasoning. The sense of class bitterness to which the party's propaganda made its principal appeal must have been magnified in many cases by personal grievances and ambitions, or by local loyalties and racial fears. And although some were no doubt deterred from joining the party by fear of persecution by the authorities or by their own friends and relations, others found in the party's sectarianism a psychological satisfaction, and willingly accepted its harsh discipline for the sake of the Calvinistic sense of 'election' which was its concomitant. Such personal factors are difficult to assess in any quantitative terms, but their general significance is attested by an ever-growing literature of ex-Communist biography.[1]

By and large, however, we may say that the early adherents of the party – those who belonged to it in the first dozen or so years of its existence – were for the most part motivated by a burning sense of hostility to class privilege and economic injustice. We have already noted the sectional factors which may have intensi- fied their preference for a new political organisation – the Jewish enthusiasm for the overthrow of Czarism in Russia, the Celtic suspicion of the existing national leadership of the labour move- ment.[2] It remains true that the Communists of the nineteen- twenties, at least after the attempts at 'Bolshevisation' had begun, were overwhelmingly proletarian in composition. Buoyed up though their activities were by Russian subsidies, the members remained individually on the verge of destitution. Frequently over half of them were unemployed, and tuberculosis seemed to be endemic among them, killing several of their leaders and crippling others. The failure of the older parties to produce any effective programme for the abolition of these social and economic evils, let alone to place such a programme on the statute book, was a powerful factor in guaranteeing the persistence of the revolution- ary organisation, tiny though it was.

In the nineteen-thirties the situation changed: to many people of all classes Communism now seemed to be the best answer to the internal and external threats of Fascism. The problems of econo- mic and social inequality were still of importance, but no longer of sole importance: and for many of the party's new recruits, the experience of poverty was more indirect than direct, involving a sense of guilt rather than an experience of suffering. Many of them were converted to Communism without ever having en- countered any of the propagandists of the British party at all: they found their new faith abroad, or by reading some left-wing writer who might not be a member of the party at all. For such persons,

[1] For an interesting analysis of the motivations of party members along these lines, see Almond, *Appeals of Communism*.

[2] The latter may be compared with the support that the French Communist Party derives from a fringe area such as Provence. See F. Goguel, *France under the Fourth Republic* (Ithaca, N.Y., 1952), p. 95.

HARRY POLLITT AND JOHN GOLLAN

the first encounter with the existing membership was often embarrassing in the extreme. But somehow the more determined of them settled down inside the party, and if they continued to find the routine activities of Communist propaganda rather unpleasant, they were often able to find compensation in special secret work suited to their talents, or in the application of Marxist theory to their own particular fields of interest.

There continued of course to be a high proportion of industrial workers in the party. Many recruits were made among the new factory population of Greater London, which included much immigrant labour from the old depressed areas. In the case of the shop stewards – the perennial opponents of trade-union officialdom – there was a natural sympathy for militant left-wing politics. But even among these elements, the fluctuations of party membership during the war had clearly come to depend primarily on the behaviour of the Soviet Union in the domestic, military and diplomatic spheres, rather than upon any factor more directly associated with the British social situation. The full employment of the post-war years has prevented any considerable revival of urgent problems in home affairs. Consequently, the gradual decline in membership totals since 1944, culminating in the crisis of 1956-7, can be closely linked with the events of the last years of Stalin's dictatorship, so far as they were known to the public, and with the handling by his successors of their awkward legacy. The remaining intellectuals in the party, who took an especially keen interest in the international scene, grew increasingly restive in this period, and chafed especially at the constant disposition of the leadership always to take its cue from the Soviet Government. Actually, this disposition was nothing like as marked as before the war, when the party had 'adopted' a Russian regiment, the Seventh (Samara) Cavalry, when its programme was entitled *For a Soviet Britain* and when intensive campaigns were carried on to familiarise the membership with the abysmal *Short History of the C.P.S.U. (Bolsheviks)*. All the same, it remained true of the post-war years that the party hardly ever deviated from the Russian 'line'. As Eric Hobsbawm pointed out early in 1957:

We tell them (*sc.* the public) that we do not give the U.S.S.R.

N

'uncritical support', but when they ask us when we disagreed with its policy, all we can point to is Nina Ponomareva's hats.[1]

The failure of the rank and file to remedy this situation in 1956–7 was due, of course, to the highly authoritarian character of the party structure, and to the fact that the existing leaders had come to power as the reliable agents of the Stalinist dictatorship.

*   *   *

It is surprising how many of the intellectuals in the party, especially those who joined in the 'anti-fascist' period or later, never realised how the structure of the party had developed in the first ten years of its existence, and how the Comintern Secretariat, by reason of its subsidies and its detailed supervision of all types of activity, had been able to transform the British Politburo to suit the whim of the Russian dictator. Needless to say, a conspiracy of silence on the part of the Pollitt-Dutt ruling clique has largely been responsible for this, and Dutt has shown himself especially anxious to limit the scope of the enquiry into the faults of Stalinism to the years since 1933.[2] But even the most outspoken of the recent rebels seem to believe that all would have been well with the party if only it had accepted Lenin and rejected Stalin, or if only it had refused to accept the imposition of the 'new line' in 1928-9.[3] In fact, however, as the history of both the Russian and the British parties shows, dictatorship was implicit in the Leninist concept of 'democratic centralism', and the British Communists put themselves entirely into the hands of the developing dictatorship of Moscow when they accepted the twenty-one theses of the Second Comintern Congress. Nothing could have emancipated them, except perhaps the attainment of power by their own efforts, as in the case of the Yugoslav and Chinese parties. But there was never the slightest prospect of this eventuality in Britain.

[1] *WN*, iv, 62.

[2] 'During this period after fascism – not previously, not therefore inherently in the system of Soviet democracy or democratic centralism – Stalin . . . began to operate new methods of working . . .' *Labour Monthly*, xxxviii, 252f.

[3] See, e.g., John Saville's introduction to 'Joseph Redman', *The Communist Party and the Labour Left, 1925-1929* (Hull, 1957), pp. 2-7.

The tradition of the British Left has tended to encourage freedom of discussion and public election of leaders inside political
organisations; and it was not easy for the little British party of the
nineteen-twenties to adapt itself to the restriction of these rights
that was involved in 'democratic centralism'. But so tight became
the grip of the Russian dictatorship on the Comintern, and
through the Comintern on the various departments and sections
of the British party, that the latter never had any opportunity of
escaping from the encroachments of authoritarianism even upon
its choice of officers. By 1929, as we have seen, the process of
'Bolshevisation' in this sphere was complete; and by 1932 or so,
when the direct subsidies from the Comintern appear to have
ceased, the party had been suitably 'conditioned', Pavlov-fashion,
to the automatic acceptance of the dictates of the Kremlin.

What were the mechanics of control inside the British party?
At first the Russian lead was transmitted to the membership, as
we have seen, through a multitude of channels, including those of
the Profintern or Red International of Labour Unions as well as
those of the Comintern. After 1934, however, the direct transmission of instructions became more intermittent, and in 1939
appears to have ceased altogether, at least until the foundation of
the Cominform. But this meant a restoration of some degree of
power, not to the party as a whole, but to its Politburo. Theoretically, of course, the Central or Executive Committee was supreme inside the party, but in practice it became a largely honorific
body, a sort of Communist 'Privy Council', too large to discuss
business efficiently[1] and useful to the real leadership primarily as a
means of rewarding party members of distinction in the outside
world with a faint semblance of authority.[2] Only on one occasion
– the outbreak of war in 1939 – was power restored to the Committee on a major issue owing to the equal balance of the opposing
members of the Politburo. But normally the Committee had no
initiative in policy and no real voice in decision-making. Its

[1] The Committee had 20 members in 1925, 30 in 1943 and 42 in 1957 – a
good example of Parkinson's Law at work.
[2] Thus the chief sub-editor of the *Daily Worker*, Allen Hutt, was co-opted
immediately after the paper had received the Newspaper Design Award.
DW, 29 Nov. 1954.

membership was to all intents and purposes selected by the Politburo, whose recommendations were accepted almost without demur by the retiring members of the Committee, by the Panels Commission of the Party Congress, and by the Congress delegates themselves.[1]

Nor was it possible for any sort of rank-and-file opposition to develop inside the party. The members were isolated inside their little locals or factory groups, and it was only very rarely that they met larger numbers of their fellow-members in aggregate meetings. Any attempt to mobilise opposition on some particular issue would run foul of the party rules, which were expressly designed to prevent the creation of 'factions'. In any case, when critical issues arose the matter was almost invariably settled by the time that the membership had an opportunity to discuss it. The decision would have been taken by the Politburo or Political Committee, and the defeated minority on this body would already have accepted the obligation to work for the approval of the majority decision by the membership. Thus the rank and file hardly ever had the opportunity to discover what the minority attitude had been, who had supported it, or what their arguments had been. Nor could anything much be done by a potential opposition at a Party Congress. The issues of the 'pre-Congress discussion' in the press were chosen by the leadership, who controlled the press; and much of the time available for discussion at the Congress itself was taken up by long-winded official reports, which took the form of finished political statements rather than hypotheses for discussion. Further, many of the important decisions of a Congress were in fact taken by its commissions, the members of which were largely chosen by those who controlled the 'higher organs' of the party. The absence of effective internal democracy was paradoxically revealed most clearly in the period of supposed liberalisation at the end of the war, when the panels system was temporarily abandoned: the membership had had no opportunity of getting to know of any suitable alternative leaders, and so had no option but to re-elect the old hands.

[1] See the evidence of Prof. George Thomson quoted in the *Report on Inner Party Democracy*, p. 55.

Under these circumstances, it is not surprising to find that over a long period the Politburo consisted substantially of the same group of officers, many of them foundation members of the party. In the thirty years beginning in 1922, when the body was instituted, we can identify only some twenty-seven men and one woman who belonged to it: almost half of them were Scotsmen, all but four or five were of working-class origin, and all but three had joined the party before 1928. Although death has taken its toll of the group, there have been few defections, and the most active survivors constitute a majority of the enlarged Political Committee of 1957. There seems to be no better guarantee of political longevity than early prominence in a revolutionary organisation – provided, of course, that there is no chance of effecting the revolution.

★   ★   ★

What, then, are we to say of the future prospects of the British Communist Party? The consolidation of the Welfare State, which we may perhaps presuppose, and the persistent, though gradual, elimination of old social barriers that will result, must continue to weaken the Communist appeal in the domestic field. For some time to come, the party may maintain a vicarious prestige by reason of the success of Communist parties in other countries, although any tendency for the spread of 'national Communism' will of course prove an embarrassment. The trend of the times is indicated by the changing character of Collet's bookshops, which in the nineteen-thirties were doing a booming trade in books and pamphlets of a directly political nature, but which in the last few years have increasingly specialised in the importation of Chinese prints and general literature from Russia and the countries of Eastern Europe. In a similar way, the Communist Party itself bids fair to become an 'agency' for the propaganda wares of the Soviet bloc nations – a 'holding company' controlling a number of organisations concerned with 'peace' and 'friendship' on Communist terms, and also possessing a few incidental 'properties' such as trade unions and professional bodies which were acquired in palmier days, but with an ever-shrinking activity of its own in its original role.

The signs of age, indeed, and of declining activities have long since begun to appear in the structure of the party. It is not merely that so many of its leading officials – Pollitt, Dutt and their contemporaries – are themselves now old men: for there is no doubt that the party will survive them. More significant indications are provided by the constant decline in the circulation of the *Daily Worker*, one of the most important aids to recruiting new members; by the wasting away of the Young Communist League, and the almost total elimination of the student Communist clubs; and, above all, by the growing unwillingness of the existing members to do more for the party than to pay an annual subscription, so that the full-time officials have to spend more and more of their time in struggling to ensure the annual re-registration of the members in their charge. These factors explain how it is that a party which still has a larger total membership today (Summer 1958) than it ever had in its first twenty years of life can yet have only a fraction of the political influence that it wielded in the pre-war years.

The fact is that a revolutionary party can become a highly conservative organisation as it grows older: it obtains property and footholds of power, which its leaders, who have also grown old, wish to retain for themselves as compensation for the loss of their youthful aspirations. These leaders are not so very different from the members of the apparently more successful 'new class' of the Communist countries, which Djilas has described so graphically:

> The once live, compact party, full of initiative, is disappearing, to become transformed into the traditional oligarchy of the new class, irresistibly drawing into its ranks those who aspire to join the new class and repressing those who have any ideals.[1]

Many of the most 'loyal' of the veterans have really lost all remnant of their faith; but they do not leave the party, for they still have things to lose if they do so – not merely their jobs, which

[1] M. Djilas, *The New Class* (1957), p. 40.

may not amount to much, but also their old friends, their way of life, and the pride which has built up in their minds through years of perseverance against the main current of public opinion.

Even if it were to make no more recruits at all, the party would still have many years to run its course. It may, indeed, yet be rescued from the fate which seems in store for it, owing to some unexpected developments in the international scene. Yet even if fate should intervene and somehow postpone the demise of this already wizened organism, we may hope that the history of its earlier years of life will become more and more a field for honest enquiry and less and less a forbidden no-man's-land, where the student is permitted to venture only at peril of bitter political controversy when his findings are presented. Venture he will, whatever the risk, if he be interested in the complexity of human motivation and political behaviour: there can be few topics more worthy of exploration than the problem of how it came to pass, that a band of British citizens could sacrifice themselves so completely over a period of almost forty years to the service of a dictatorship in another country, and could find it so difficult to adjust themselves to the revelation of the dictator's all too human imperfections.

Appendix A

OFFICIAL FIGURES OF PARTY MEMBERSHIP

Date	*Total*	*Source*
1922	5116, but fees for only 2300	ECCI, *Fourth Congress Report* (1922), p. 289.
1924	4000 ⎫	*C.I. Between 5th and 6th World Congress*
1925	5000 ⎬	(1928), p. 30.
1926 (Apr.)	6000 ⎭	
(Oct.)	10730	CP *8th Congress Report*, p. 39.
1927 (Oct.)	7377	*Inprecorr*, vii, 1288.
1929 (Jan.)	3500	*Communist Review*, iv, 383.
(Dec.)	3200	*Inprecorr*, xii, 446.
1930 (Nov.)	2555	*Ibid.*, xi, 680.
1931 (June)	2724 ⎫	*Ibid.*, xii, 447.
(Nov.)	6279 ⎭	
1932 (Jan.)	9000	*Communist Review*, iv, 383.
(Nov.)	5600	*Ibid.*, p. 577.
1934 (Dec.)	5800 ⎫	*Inprecorr*, xv, 1053.
1935 (July)	7700 ⎭	
1936 (Oct.)	11500	*Discussion*, Nov. 1936, p. 12.
1937 (May)	12250	*DW*, 27 May 1937.
1938 (Sept.)	15570	*DW*, 19 Sept. 1938.
1939 (July)	17756	*Report of C.C. to 16th Congress*, p. 13.
1941 (Dec.)	22738	*WNV*, xxii, 206.
1942 (Dec.)	56000	*WNV*, xxiii, 221.
1943 (Dec.)	55138	*WNV*, xxiv, 63.
1945 (Mar.)	45435	*Report of E.C. to 18th Congress*, p. 17.
1946 (Apr.)	42123	*WNV*, xxvi, 198.
1947 (June)	38579	*WNV*, xxviii, 99.
1948 (Apr.)	43000	*DW*, 1 May 1948.
1950 (May)	38853 ⎫	*Report of E.C. to 22nd Congress*, p. 17.
1952 (Mar.(	35124 ⎭	
1953 (Mar.)	35054	*Report of E.C. to 23rd Congress*, p. 12.

Date	*Total*	*Source*
1954 (Apr.)	33963 ⎫	
1955 (Mar.)	32681 ⎬	*For a Lasting Peace* . . . 13 Apr. 1956.
1956 (Feb.)	33095 ⎭	
1957 (Feb.)	26742	*WN*, iv, 149. 13 Apr. 1956.
1958 (Feb.)	24670	*DW*, 11 Feb. 1958.

Appendix B

PARTY CONGRESSES

First (Unity)	July	1920	London (City)
Second (Unity)	Jan.	1921	Leeds
Third (Rules)	Apr.	1921	Manchester
Fourth (Policy)	Mar.	1922	London (St. Pancras)
Fifth	Oct.	1922	London (Battersea)
Sixth	May	1924	Manchester
Seventh	May	1925	Glasgow
Eighth	Oct.	1926	London (Battersea)
Ninth	Oct.	1927	Salford
Tenth	Jan.	1929	London (Bermondsey)
Eleventh (Special)	Nov.	1929	Leeds
Twelfth	Nov.	1932	London (Battersea)
Thirteenth	Feb.	1935	Manchester
Fourteenth	May	1937	London (Battersea)
Fifteenth	Sept.	1938	Birmingham
Sixteenth	July	1943	London (City)
Seventeenth	Oct.	1944	Birmingham
Eighteenth	Nov.	1945	London (Marylebone)
Nineteenth	Feb.	1947	London (Marylebone)
Twentieth	Feb.	1948	London (Marylebone)
Twenty-First	Nov.	1949	Liverpool
Twenty-Second	Apr.	1952	London (Battersea)
Twenty-Third	Apr.	1954	London (Battersea)
Twenty-Fourth	Apr.	1956	London (Battersea)
Twenty-Fifth (Special)	Apr.	1957	London (Hammersmith)

INDEX

Acton, 118f, 132f
Adamson, William, 88
Aitken, George, 114
Albania, 150
Allan, Willie, 66, 71f
Allison, George, 41
All Power, 27
America, United States of, 2, 78, 107, 134, 143f, 162, 168; Congress, 122; Dept. of State, 171f
'Amsterdam International', *see* International Federation of Trade Unions
Anarcho-Syndicalists (of Spain), 91
Anglo-Russian Joint Council, 34
Anglo-Soviet Mutual Aid Pact (1941), 119
Anti-semitism, 16, 82f, 88, 129, 167f, 173, 175, 179
Arab seamen, 70
Aragon, 92, 93
'Arcos', 43f
Arnot, R. Page, 17, 51, 52, 56n
Artists for Peace, 146
Attlee, C. R., 93, 115, 141
Auden, W. H., 80f
Authors' World Peace Appeal, 146

Bakunin, M., 135
Barishnik, 57
Battersea, North, 25, 31
Beaverbrook, Lord, 143
Behan, Brian, 179, 181
Belgrade, 148, 160n
Bell, Tom, 4, 7, 23, 46, 51, 52, 89
Bennett, Mick, 168
Beria, L. P., 168
Berlin, 42, 153
Bevan, Aneurin, 98f
Bevin, Ernest, 5, 137, 140, 141, 153
Birkenhead, 65
Birmingham, 132
Blackburn, 63
'Black Circular' (1934), 84, 105, 135
Blanesburgh Report (1927), 64
Blum, Leon, 98

'Bolshevisation', 23, 47, 183, 187
Bond, R. E., 41
Bondfield, Margaret, 64
Borodin, Michael, 21, 28
Bournemouth, 134
Bradford, 62
Bradley, Ben, 41, 117f
Bramley, Ted, 118, 132
Bright, Frank, 61f
British Broadcasting Corporation (B.B.C.), 165
British-China Friendship Association, 145
British Cultural Committee for Peace, 146
British-Czechoslovak Friendship League, 145
British Empire, 41, 48, 161, 182
British Labour and Communism, 88
British Peace Committee, 146
British-Polish Society, 145
'British Road to Socialism', 161, 171
British-Rumanian Friendship Association, 145
British Socialist Party (B.S.P.), 3, 4, 5, 7-10, 15, 124
British-Soviet Friendship Society, *see* Friends of the Soviet Union
British-Vietnam Committee, 145
British Youth Festival Committee, 146
British-Yugoslav Association, 145, 150f
Brockway, Fenner, 78, 98
Browder, Earl, 134
Brown, Ernie, 62
Brown, George, 93
Brown, W. J., 157
Brunete, 93
Builders Forward Movement, 72
Bukharin, N., 45, 100
Bulganin, N., 169
Bulgaria, 145, 150
Burgess, Guy, 162
Burns, Emile, 109, 166
Burnley, 62, 63
Busmen's Rank and File Movement, 86

200

INDEX

Miners Federation, *later* National Union of Mineworkers (N.U.M.), 34, 35, 153f
Mineworkers of Scotland, United, 56, 57, 69, 85, 88
Minority Movement, 38, 49, 55, 156; founded (1923-4), 27; Moscow control of, 32, 57f, 69-72; activities of, 56f, 60, 62f, 66; dissolved (1933), 72.
Modern Quarterly, 81, 165, 166
Moffat, Alex, 174
Morgan, T. H., 165
Morris, William, 1, 2
Morrison, Herbert, 88, 117, 121, 125
Moscow Narodny Bank in London, 43
Mosley, Sir Oswald, 82, 88, 129
Motherwell, 25
Münzenberg, Willi, 38, 42, 148
Murphy, J. T., 7, 16, 23, 24f, 50, 68
Musicians' Organisation for Peace, 146
Mutiny Act (1797), 34

Napier aircraft works, Acton, 118f
National Assembly of Women, 146
National Association of Labour Student Organisations, 139
National Council of Civil Liberties, 115, 129, 156, 157
National Council of Labour, 88
'National' Government (1931-40), 67, 73, 92, 112, 116
National Health Service, 138
National Left Wing Movement, 40f, 55
National Transport Workers Federation, 19
National Unemployed Workers' (Committee) Movement (N.U.W.M.), 26, 39, 57, 63-65, 66, 102
National Union of Students, 115
Nazism (National Socialism) *and* Nazis, 65, 73, 75, 79, 82, 89, 91, 110
Newbold, Walton, 13, 17, 25
New Leader, 55
New Reasoner, 181
News Chronicle, 103
New Statesman, 175, 181
New York, 49, 67
Nin, A., 27
Nonconformity, 62
Normandy, invasion of (1944), 129
'Nucleus', 22, 25, 37, 51

Olympia Fascist meeting (1934), 82f
Organisation for the Maintenance of Supplies, 34
Orwell, George, 99, 104
Oxford, 106

Paine, Tom, 1
'Panel' system of election, 52, 59, 103, 130, 133, 160, 176f, 188
Pankhurst, Sylvia, 6, 7f, 9, 10, 11, 12, 13, 19f
Papworth, Bert, 86, 136, 154, 155
Paris, 92
Parkinson's Law, 187n
Paul, William, 10, 40
People's Convention (1941), 116f
People's Press Printing Society, 139
Petrovsky, D., 28, 41, 54, 100
Phillips, Morgan, 153
Piatakov, Y., 100
Pieck, W., 122
Piratin, Phil, 83, 131, 163
'Pitcairn, Frank', *see* Cockburn, Claud
Plebs League, 3, 22
Poland, 110, 173f
Polish forces in Britain, 129
Polish Government, 112
Political Commissars, 93f
Pollitt, Harry: 'Bolshevises' C.P.G.B., 21, 23f; manages Minority Movement, 27; Moscow confidence in, 49; becomes general secretary (1929), 52; consolidates power, 68; as 'leader', 89; criticises party's industrial work, 56, 69, 70; supports Soviet trials, 100, 101; supports war (1939), 110-2, 114; temporarily out of office, 113; supports Cominform line, 142, 149f, 167f, 174; modifies views (1956), 170; becomes chairman, 171; Parliamentary contests of, 87, 131f, 163; visits abroad – to U.S.A., 49, 78; to U.S.S.R., 54f, 169, 172; to India, 182n; other references, 88, 94, 119, 134, 178, 180, 181, 186, 190
Pontecorvo, Bruno, 16
Ponomareva, Nina, 186
'Popular Front', 76, 98f, 164
Postgate, Raymond, 17, 22
Post-War History of the British Working Class (Hutt), 89f